Joachim Remak is Professor of History at the University of California, Santa Barbara. He is the author of numerous books and articles on modern European history, including *Sarajevo: The Story of a Political Murder*, *The First World War: Causes, Conduct, Consequences*; and *The Nazi Years: A Documentary History*.

EUROPE 1919

NEW INDEPENDENT NATIONS

ALLIED OCCUPATION ZONE
(British, French, American)

0   100   200   300 miles

NORWAY

SWEDEN

Gulf of Bothnia

FINLAND

Ladoga

Helsinki

Petrograd

Oslo

Stockholm

Tallin

ESTONIA

North Sea

Baltic Sea

Riga

LATVIA

U.S.S.R.

DENMARK

Copenhagen

Memel

LITHUANIA

Danzig

Kaunas

NETHERLANDS

Hamburg

Elbe

Berlin

EAST PRUSSIA

Amsterdam

BELGIUM

Brussels

GERMANY

Leipzig

Vistula

Warsaw

Cologne

LUX.

Coblenz

Oder

POLAND

SAAR

Mainz

Dresden

Kiev

Dnieper

50°

FRANCE

Rhine

Prague

Cracow

Munich

CZECHOSLOVAKIA

Danube

SWITZERLAND

AUSTRIA

Vienna

Budapest

Geneva

HUNGARY

Milan

ROMANIA

Odessa

Marseilles

Belgrade

Bucharest

ITALY

Adriatic Sea

YUGOSLAVIA

Danube

Black Sea

Rome

Sofia

BULGARIA

Naples

Tirana

Constantinople

40°

ALBANIA

GREECE

TURKEY

Aegean Sea

Mediterranean Sea

30°

JOACHIM REMAK

THE ORIGINS
OF THE SECOND
WORLD WAR

A SPECTRUM BOOK

PRENTICE-HALL, INC., Englewood Cliffs, New Jersey

Library of Congress Cataloging in Publication Data
Remak, Joachim
    The origins of World War II.

    (A Spectrum book)
    Bibliography: p.
        1. World War, 1939–1945—Causes.   2. World War,
1939–1945—Sources.   3. Europe—History—1918–1945—
Sources.   I. Title.
    D741.R38   940.53'11   75-30687
    ISBN 0-13-642751-0
    ISBN 0-13-642744-8 pbk.

© 1976 by Prentice-Hall, Inc., Englewood Cliffs, New Jersey

A Spectrum Book

10 9 8 7 6 5 4 3 2 1

Printed in the United States of America

Prentice-Hall International, Inc., *London*
Prentice-Hall of Australia Pty. Ltd., *Sydney*
Prentice-Hall of Canada, Ltd., *Toronto*
Prentice-Hall of India Private Limited, *New Delhi*
Prentice-Hall of Japan, Inc., *Tokyo*
Prentice-Hall of Southeast Asia (Pte.) Ltd., *Singapore*

FOR BOB AND CATHY

Europe is confronted with a program of aggression, nicely calculated and timed, unfolding stage by stage, and there is only one choice open . . . either to submit . . . or to take effective measures while time remains to ward off the danger, and if it cannot be worked off, to cope with it.

WINSTON CHURCHILL

March 14, 1938

I shall not give up the hope of a peaceful solution, or abandon my efforts for peace, as long as any chance for peace remains.

NEVILLE CHAMBERLAIN

September 27, 1938.

Contents

Preface

Two world wars changed our century and our lives. The first was the result of accident as much as of design. The second was the just about perfect model of a planned war. Together, they caused the deaths of more people than all preceding continental wars, and all natural disasters since the discovery of the New World. Yet both were quite avoidable wars. There were many turns in the road that might have led away from the precipice.

But that is speculation. This book shows how Europe and the world did move from one war to the next. It does so in two ways: First, an essay chapter provides an overview, recounting how in the space of hardly more than twenty years, from 1918 to 1939, one war was allowed to lead to another. This is followed by some documentary chapters, in which the sources from which historians construct their accounts are allowed to speak for themselves, giving a sharper perception of the truth than most narratives can.

Both in the essay and in the documentary parts, the author/editor has had the help of several people. They are Nicolay Altankov, Morton Borden, Harold Drake, Otis Graham, Steven Leibo, Bruce Loynd, Kim Street, and Robert Young, all at the University of California at Santa Barbara, and Lynne Lumsden at Prentice-Hall. They have suggested documents for inclusion that would have escaped him; they have provided ideas and approaches that did not occur to him, and prevented mistakes that did. In thanking them here, far more than a routine debt is being acknowledged—this is their book, too.

PART 1

THE COMING OF ANOTHER WORLD WAR, AN ESSAY

End/Results of war
Treaty Versailles I
current circumstance
conducive to war

THE HOPEFUL TWENTIES

How could Europe, twenty years after the carnage of the First World War engage in another, and even bloodier conflict? The one-word answer often given—and it can still be heard today—is Versailles. It was the victor's peace of 1919 that bore the seeds of a second great war—the treaty imposed by the Allies on the defeated powers, a treaty that robbed them of territory, humiliated them with a spurious, or at least arguable, war guilt clause, and mortgaged their economies with an unprecedented bill for reparations. No wonder then that in one form or another, all the defeated nations made the Hungarian slogan of *"nem, nem, soha!"* their own. "No, no, never!" Or, as Marshal Foch, prophet before the event, put it in 1919: "This is not a peace. It is an armistice for twenty years."

The explanation, then, is a tempting one. But it will not stand up under any real examination of the evidence. It will not for two major reasons. One is that too much was right with the first decade or so that followed the Peace of Paris, that too many of the war's wounds were healed. The other is that Versailles was pretext rather than motive in 1939, and that the nation that would begin World War II was pursuing aims that went far beyond those of righting the wrongs of 1919.

Let us, therefore, begin with a brief survey of the 1920s and of the hopes that that decade engendered among reasonable and normally cautious men. And after that, let us take a somewhat longer look at the shattering of these hopes in the thirties, at the challenge of aggression, and the response of the democracies. Together, those two topics will provide as good a guide as any through the diplomacy, public and private, of the between-the-wars period and show why war would come again while the living could still remember the dead of Ypres and Verdun.

3

YEARS OF HOPE: LEAGUE, LOCARNO,
BRIAND–KELLOGG (1919–1931)

LEAGUE OF NATIONS AND
INTERNATIONAL COURT OF JUSTICE

Few institutions have been as consistently attacked, by amateurs and experts alike, as the League of Nations. It failed in its major function, that of preserving the peace. It failed in its more limited functions as well, such as the sponsorship of disarmament or the protection of minorities (whether of Armenians in Turkey or of Magyars in Rumania or of Jews in Poland). But the element of hindsight in these judgments is too strong. For while it was perfectly clear after 1936, after the failure of sanctions against Fascist Italy, that the League was not a serious factor in international affairs, a considerably more cheerful view was possible in the twenties, and any survey of those years ought to begin with a look at Woodrow Wilson's creation, and what was right with it.

What was right with the League, to begin with, was its very existence. The world's powers, major and minor, now regularly met at Geneva. America, it was true, was missing, and so, for the first few years, were Russia and Germany. Still, those who came far outnumbered those who stayed away. A great forum thus was available for the public airing of grievances and for the private settling of differences. And differences *were* settled. Wars that do not take place, by definition, attract less attention than those that do. Hence few people remember that the League arranged for the peaceful resolution of at least two great crises in the early twenties, one between Greece and Bulgaria over a border incident, and another between Sweden and Finland over the possession of a group of Baltic islands. In addition, the League acted as a mediator in dozens of less grave disputes, in the Middle East, in South America, and elsewhere.

The words "great crises" seem inappropriate. What difference did it make whose flag was flying over the Aland Islands? Or would a Greek-Bulgarian border clash, if left unresolved, really have caused a war? The answer is that it might have. The crisis that culminated in World War I had begun over less.

The League also did some splendid work through its technical agencies, from the data collected by the International Labor Organization to the worldwide control of the drug trade. Above all, however, there was established under League auspices, in 1921, a Permanent Court of International Justice at The Hague. The Court was not an entirely new creation; rather, it went back in origin to the Permanent Court of Arbitration established by the First Hague Peace Conference in 1899. But the powers and functions of the new court went beyond those of its predecessor. All members of the League agreed to submit international disputes in which they might be involved to the Court for arbitration. They also agreed to abide by the Court's decision if it were to be unanimously endorsed by the League Council, and accepted by the other party, or parties, to the disputes. The reservations were important ones, yet there did now exist in Europe a supranational authority to which disputes could be submitted for adjudication. Here was a workable alternative to war. And during the next two decades, some sixty cases would be submitted to the International Court. In each instance, the contesting parties were to accept and honor the Court's finding.

THE WASHINGTON NAVAL CONFERENCE (1921–1922)

Many a dispute, of course, never was submitted to the Court; the bad old ways of using political or economic pressure to achieve one's aims had by no means lost their attraction. But soon after the war, a major step forward was taken in a matter perennially more talked about than acted on—disarmament. In the winter of 1921 to 1922, the world's leading naval powers met at Washington, where, after much debate, they reached two significant agreements. One was to declare a building holiday for capital ships; for a ten-year period, no new battleships or heavy cruisers were to be constructed. The other was to establish a ratio of capital ships between the United States, Great Britain, Japan, France, and Italy of 5:5:3:1.75:1.75. The precise figures may sound abstract today; their significance should not. For by establishing, in advance, a clear and predictable relation between the nations' naval strength, they effectively reduced the temptation to engage in any new arms race at sea.

RAPALLO (1922)

These agreements were among the victors. But there took place, also in 1922, a diplomatic event that brought a major loser out of isolation. In the spring of that year, at the Italian resort town of Rapallo, the government of Germany signed an agreement with that of the Soviet Union. In it, the two countries re-established diplomatic relations, renounced all reparations claims that either side might have against the other, and pledged their cooperation in the economic sphere.

Not all writers have described Rapallo as an indication of Europe's new health; in fact, the thought of Germany's turning east—then or now—still strikes some as ominous. And it is true that following Rapallo, the Russians, surreptitiously and in violation of the provisions of Versailles, offered training facilities to some German military specialists. Yet their number was small; the purpose of Rapallo was neither to train a new German air force in the East nor to terrify the West with a grand new Russo-German alliance. Both nations were far too weak for that at the time. The purpose of Rapallo, rather, was to let both powers break out of their isolation, which had been imposed on one by its having lost the war, and on the other by its having won a revolution. If the Western nations would not speak to Germany or Russia, except to present more bills for the war, the Russians and the Germans might as well do some talking with each other. Who knew, the conversation might become more general before long. And so it did. Rapallo would succeed in its basic purpose. And while it would be a challenge, or in pre-Toynbee terms, an annoyance to the West, no European recovery, no European peace, was possible while Germany and Russia remained in limbo. Neither of them, after all, could be expelled from the Continent.

LOCARNO (1925)

Initially, the challenge of Rapallo merely provoked a sharper anti-German attitude on the part of France. But that attitude led nowhere. France's wartime ally, Great Britain, had no more taste for perpetuating the resentments of the war than for seeing the potential hegemony of Germany over Europe replaced by that of France. There are certain constants in history and in international affairs, and one of the constants of British foreign policy was a preference for a balance of power. Let no one power dominate the Continent, lest it become a threat to peace, and to Britain. It had in large part been for the balance of power that Britain had gone to war in 1914; it was the same concept that now made Britain oppose the anti-German line taken by France. And British opposition coincided with a new French understanding of the nature of the German problem. Germany, it became apparent to Paris, was too vital a country to control with force or threats of force for any length of time. Sooner or later, cooperation would have to replace coercion.

In 1925, that new mood was translated into a concrete agreement, signed at the Swiss town of Locarno. Under the terms of the treaty, France, Belgium, and Germany agreed on a mutual guarantee of their existing borders, with Great Britain and Italy agreeing to act as guarantors—which meant that in case of any violations of Locarno, they would come to the aid of the aggrieved party. That this could only mean to the aid of France or possibly Belgium was perfectly clear, since no one but the Germans had any territorial grievances here. But few anticipated any need for such action, for the great significance of the treaty was that the Germans, voluntarily and without the threat of occupation and blockade as in 1919, recognized the verdict of Versailles. Here, then, was a new beginning and a new spirit. A year later, in 1926, Germany, the pariah of 1919, was admitted to full membership in the League of Nations.

KELLOGG–BRIAND: THE PACT OF PARIS (1928)

Locarno was followed, in 1928, by an even more far-reaching agreement. Its formal name was the Pact of Paris, although it would usually be referred to as the Kellogg-Briand pact, after its two principal authors, the American Secretary of State and the foreign minister of France. The treaty, before long, was signed by most of the world's powers. Its text was brief, its essential paragraphs no more than two:

Article 1. The High Contracting Parties solemnly declare in the names of their respective peoples that they condemn recourse to war for the solution of international controversies and renounce it as an instrument of national policy in their relations with one another.

Article 2. The High Contracting Parties agree that the settlement or solution of all disputes or conflicts of whatever nature or of whatever origin they may be, which may arise among them, shall never be sought except by pacific means.

No quarrel between nations ought ever again be worth the risk of ten million dead.

The Spirit of Locarno (1928–1930)

There was other evidence of returning sanity, and of conciliation. The French agreed to withdraw what remained of their occupation troops from the Rhineland some years ahead of the schedule established at Versailles, and by 1930, the last of the Allied troops had left German soil. Reparations were eased, in a number of compromise measures that, it was true, were attributable more to American than to French initiative, but to which all sides agreed. Above all, there was a very great deal of material prosperity in Europe. No one could say which came first, but good feelings internationally did go with high employment domestically. The Germans, ten years after Versailles, were sending a Zeppelin around the world. The French, that same year, despite the fact that the term "Western front" had meant the French front, saw their industrial production overtake that of 1914 by 40 percent.

Was everything, then, in good order in the twenties? Of course it was not. There were Germans who preferred being indignant over Versailles to rejoicing over the flight of the dirigible. There were Frenchmen who never forgave the *boche.* In 1923, when the Germans defaulted on their reparations payments, French troops would occupy Germany's industrial heartland, the Ruhr, for two years. Nor would every last Frenchman feel secure even after Locarno and Kellogg-Briand. Some of Germany's eastern neighbors were worried because there never was a Locarno treaty for them. Arbitration treaties between Germany and Poland, and Germany and Czechoslovakia, were signed at Locarno; and in subsequent years, the files of the various ministries would grow heavy with *projects* for a grand settlement in the East, yet there never would be a clear guarantee of these borders. Of course all the powers had abjured war—but how was Kellogg-Briand to be enforced? What was to be the penalty for breaking it? The treaty did not say. And the two principal architects of German-French understanding, Gustav Stresemann and Aristide Briand, died much too early; Stresemann in 1929, Briand in 1932.

Then there was the American retreat into isolation, and the falling out between the two major European victors, Britain and France. England, her territory undamaged in the war, and, by virtue of Europe's geography, fairly immune from invasion, reverted to her traditional policy of opposing the supremacy of *any* power on the continent. Hence Britain was ready to rediscover certain desirable qualities in the enemy of yesterday, the principal such quality being that he might be of help against the enemy of tomorrow. (Thus the British opposed France's occupation of the Ruhr, and effectively so. The French would have to leave without having achieved their objective.) France, on the other hand, favored a much harder line, at least in the immediate postwar period. "Twenty million Germans too many" was French Premier Clemenceau's phrase. A rhetorical exaggeration? Hardly so, at least not from a certain French point of view. France had won the war, yet there were 39 million Frenchmen in 1918, and 63 million Germans. And no channel separated the 63 million from France.

Yet on balance, Versailles, at the end of the twenties, was a memory and not a policy. The British were ready for peace. The French, while they were not ready to love the Germans, were prepared to live with them. "If you cannot have what you like you must like what you have," an eminent French prewar diplomat had written apropos of the Russians. It was good advice still. And the Germans, some irreconcilables aside, a decade after the war had occasion to recall the words of their greatest nineteenth-century novelist, Theodor Fontane. "All states must regain the courage of not being frightened by defeat. An occasional defeat does not harm a people—neither its honor nor its happiness. On the contrary, the opposite is often true. The defeated nation must only have the strength to rise again on its own resources. In that case, it is happier, richer, more powerful than before."

They were not quite that, yet, but the war was past. It was not until the 1930s that things would go wrong, mildly at first, and then very wrong indeed.

YEARS OF DANGER: THE THIRTIES

Three major developments made the thirties very different from the decade that had preceded it. The first was the depression, the second was the reappearance of old-fashioned aggression as practiced by Japan and Italy, and the third was the new and startling kind of aggression practiced by Adolf Hitler.

all these were circumstances conducive to war

THE YEARS OF THE ANTIS:
LONDON TO GENEVA (1930–1932)

The great depression that started in the United States in 1929 and soon thereafter turned into a worldwide phenomenon introduced a mood of irritability and pettiness into the conduct of European diplomacy. Nothing seemed to go right any more. In 1930, the powers met in London to discuss naval disarmament. Might not the principles of the Washington agreement of 1922 logically and fruitfully be extended to non-capital ships? It was a constructive idea, and there was much talk, and nothing came of it. Nor did the Geneva disarmament conference of 1932 achieve any more. It was more ambitious in scope; land as well as naval armaments were on its schedule. What wrecked it was the new mood plus the revival of an old one—Franco-German antagonism. In 1932, the Germans had effectively halted all reparations payments. The United States and Great Britain showed some readiness to reconcile themselves to what seemed to them inevitable; the French did not. And that same year, in part to cope with the depression, in part to pursue some grander policy aims, the Germans had entered into a customs union with Austria. The French blocked the move, or rather they submitted it to the International Court at The Hague, which ruled that it violated the provisions of the Paris peace treaties that had specifically outlawed any Austro-German union.

The spirit of Locarno was dead.

THE CHALLENGE OF AGGRESSION, MANCHURIA TO MUNICH (1931–1938)

Before long, the failure of the disarmament talks would look relatively harmless. Those were the good old days when all that was at stake were some technical disagreements among the experts at Geneva. Events now were taking place—in Asia, Europe, and Africa—that threatened the survival of peace itself.

To provide some intelligible guide through these events, to show the pattern and not just the detail, it may be best to consider three topics, and to consider them separately. The first will be a brief chronicle of events, from 1931 to 1938, or from Manchuria to Munich, as seen from the point of view of the aggressors. The second is the response of the West to that aggression. And the third will be the motives of both sides, the true motives, not the public ones. It will be the longest of the three topics, since it is the motives that will provide the clue to what went wrong in the end.

The new violence began in Asia. In 1931, Japan invaded the Chinese province of Manchuria. It seemed a worthwhile prize. It offered just about all the rewards of imperialist venture—a region that could absorb some of the surplus population of an overcrowded land, and that held high promise for capital investment as well; a neglected, underdeveloped province whose growth potential seemed immense, and that, all economic considerations aside, would be a strategic outpost against the Soviet Union. And both prestige and profit could be wrested from a weak opponent. The Chinese, as Tokyo had foreseen, could put up no effective defense. Within a matter of weeks, the Japanese conquest of Manchuria was complete. Early in 1932, Manchuria became the nominally independent Republic of Manchukuo, with a former emperor of China as head of state. Nominally independent, that is, for it was perfectly clear who controlled the new country.

The new challenge to the status quo came in Europe. In 1933, Adolf Hitler was appointed chancellor of Germany. His publicly proclaimed policy was peace. Versailles was a shameful treaty, he said, and "every problem that causes unrest today goes back to the defects of the Peace Treaty," but he added that he had no desire for another holocaust. In fact, he was ready to offer certain proposals toward disarmament, provided only that they were accepted on the non-Versailles basis of German equality. When, as he had anticipated, there was no French response to that, he took Germany out of the Geneva disarmament conference, and out of the League of Nations as well. The nation would not return to either organization, he said, until it was assured of a fully equal status. "The German government and the German people are determined to endure every distress, every persecution and every hardship rather than to sign any more treaties that would be intolerable to any man of honor, . . . and which would merely perpetuate the fear and the misery produced by the Treaty of Versailles."

The date was October 1933. Hitler's next, and logical, step came a year and a half later, when, in March 1935, he publicly denounced the clauses of the Versailles treaty that limited German armaments. Henceforth, he said, the army's size would be determined not by what the victors at Paris had allowed it but by what the Germans wished it to be. For the time being, that would be in the neighborhood of half a million men. (Versailles had laid down a maximum of 100,000.) Nor would the nation feel bound any longer by the restrictions on the size of its navy. And Germany would have an air force once more. In fact, it already had one. It had been secretly built up at Hitler's orders and about equaled Great Britain's in power.

Open aggression came next. It was instigated not by Hitler, who could wait a while now, but by his ally, Mussolini. In the fall of 1935, the Duce ordered the Italian armed forces to invade Ethiopia, last of the independent African kingdoms. Italy wished to expand; Italy wished revenge for the great defeat imposed on it by Ethiopian troops at the end of the nineteenth century. Besides, it was "a war of civilization and liberty," said Mussolini, and "a test of our virility." It certainly *was* a test of the superiority of guns and planes and poison gas over spears and arrows. Early in 1936, the Ethiopians were forced to surrender. The emperor, Haile Selassie, went into exile; Italian troops entered Addis Ababa, Ethiopia's capital. "Civilization," said Mussolini, "has triumphed over barbarism." (In the 1960 Olympics, the route of the marathon race ended with a re-entry into Rome under the Arch of Constantine, and thence into the Olympic Stadium, where the words DUCE DUCE DUCE could still be seen engraved in the marble. The race was won by an Ethiopian soldier. And in 1970, Emperor Haile Selassie, very sovereign once more, would visit Rome, be received both by the pope and by the president of Italy and terminate the state visit by laying a wreath at the tomb of the Unknown Italian Soldier. But we are getting ahead of our story here.)

Civilization next marched on the Franco-German border. In March 1936, German troops reoccupied the part of the Rhineland that had been demilitarized under the terms of Versailles. The treaty's ban on placing either troops or military installations in the area was no longer binding, said Hitler, and for good measure he repudiated the Locarno treaty as well.

It seemed time for Europe's two most active, and fascist, of powers to join forces. So they did, forming, at the end of 1936, not just an old-fashioned alliance but an ideological, political, and diplomatic partnership. It would be an Axis, said Mussolini, "an Axis around which can revolve all those European states with a will to collaboration and peace."

The fascist interpretation of these terms became apparent in the Spanish Civil War opening that year between Franco's Nationalists and the forces of the Spanish Republican government. Both Axis nations actively supported Franco. The greater part of the support came from Italy—arms, general supplies, and some 50,000 troops. The German contribution, while smaller, included a crack tank battalion and a small air force, the *Legion Condor*. And Axis aid was crucial. Without it, the Republican forces would very likely have defeated Franco's by the end of 1936. As it was, the government side now sought foreign aid as well, and while none was forthcoming from Britain and France, the Soviet Union did send a number of advisors and technicians—never more than 500 at any given point—and a modest amount of material aid. Also, opponents of fascism the world over organized an International Brigade. Its members were to fight, and die, on many fronts. Of 10,000 French volunteers—the largest single national contingent—about 3,000 were killed; of some 5,000 anti-Nazi German and Austrian volunteers, perhaps 2,000 died in battle. But ultimately, neither the International Brigade nor Russian aid could save the Republic, and in the spring of 1939 Madrid surrendered, and with that surrender, all resistance in effect collapsed. Franco had won, with the help of the Axis, and at the cost of perhaps three-quarters of a million Spanish lives.

Yet it had, in spite of foreign aid, military and financial, been essentially a *Spanish* civil war, understandable mainly in terms of

Spanish politics and of Spain's past. Axis intervention had to a large extent been fortuitous. Aiding one side or the other on the Iberian peninsula had been no part of Hitler's grand design. But there took place, in the spring of 1938, an event that very much was a part of it—the invasion of Austria.

The ban on union between Germany and Austria that had been a part of the Paris peace meant nothing to the Austrian-born Hitler. "Common blood," he had written on the first page of *Mein Kampf*, "belongs in a common Reich." An earlier attempt at a German-directed Nazi coup, undertaken in 1934, had failed, but in 1938 he felt strong enough to act again. "Over ten million Germans live in two of the states adjoining our borders," he said in February of that year. "The protection of those German people is among the interests of the German Reich." In March, he was ready to protect them to the fullest. Under intense pressure from Berlin, the legal Austrian government ceded power to a group of Austrian Nazis, who thereupon sent a telegram to Berlin inviting German troops into the country "to restore law and order." It was a rather special telegram. The text was telephoned from Berlin to the new authorities in Vienna, who then wired it back to Berlin, for the record. But the subsequent German invasion of Austria was equally special—it was a peaceful, even a joyous affair. It became known as the flower campaign; no other projectiles struck the invaders. An overwhelming majority of Austrians welcomed union with the Reich, as did most Germans. In April, an ecstatic Hitler addressed a like-minded crowd in Vienna. "I believe it was God's will to send a youth from here into the Reich, to let him grow up, to raise him to be the leader of the nation in order to enable him to lead his homeland back into the Reich. . . . May every German recognize the hour and measure its import and bow in humility before the Almighty, who in a few weeks has wrought a miracle upon us!"

"Ten million Germans." "Two of the states." The miracle was not yet complete. There remained the Czechoslovak Republic with its 3,000,000 ethnic Germans living in the Sudeten area that bordered on Germany. Hitler now gave them his full attention. The German press played up instances of Czech oppression, alleged and real. A Sudeten German Nazi movement received increasingly active support from Berlin. They should always, Hitler instructed them, demand just so much from the Prague government that the Czechs must still negotiate with them, but never so little that their demands might be granted. What was needed was crisis—and a man to resolve it. And in the fall of 1938, he told the world that he was that man, and that he was impatient to act. He was demanding self-determination for the Sudeten Germans, he said in a speech violent even for him, and he was demanding it now.

The speech was followed by even bloodier disorders in Czechoslovakia. Hitler's response was to announce that he was no longer prepared to see Germans persecuted. He was resolved, he said, on settling the issue "in one way or another." He wished the West to understand that he was a man of reason, however. All he intended to do was to liberate his fellow Germans, not to annex any ethnic undesirables. "We want no Czechs!"

[handwritten marginalia: reason / try to seem nice]

There were those who had their reservations about that assurance, but the meaning of "in one way or another" was perfectly clear. In an effort to avoid catastrophe, the British prime minister, Neville Chamberlain, made two trips to Germany that fall. Did not, he asked Hitler, some basis of agreement still exist? At the end of September, these preliminary conversations were followed by a larger conference of the leaders of Great Britain, France, Italy, and Germany at Munich, during which just about all of Hitler's public demands were met. Prague was forced to cede the entire Sudeten area to Germany, to hand another, smaller, area in the North to Poland, and to grant autonomy to Slovakia.

[handwritten marginalia: not a threat]

Ten million Germans had joined the Reich.

THE RESPONSE OF THE WEST, MANCHURIA TO MUNICH.

But it is time to interrupt the narrative of events as seen from the aggressors' side and to consider the reaction of the supposed guardians of the peace in the West. It can be done in fairly few words; the summing up is simple enough. The West acted helpless in the face of treaties repudiated and of promises broken, and countered aggression with words, not acts.

Thus, in the Manchurian case, Japan had to face nothing more terrifying than some verbal condemnation. British and French editorial writers disapproved of Japan's course. And the United States declared that it would take no legal cognizance of it. Washington, said the American Secretary of State, Henry L.

Stimson, would not recognize this or in fact any other conquest achieved by force of arms. (The policy of diplomatic nonrecognition became known as the Stimson Doctrine; the Japanese found it bearable.) The League of Nations appointed a commission of inquiry, which a year later announced its finding. It was that Japan had been the aggressor. Few had thought otherwise, though the verdict sufficiently annoyed the Japanese to make them quit the League.

Nor did the West react any more effectively to Hitler. His successive repudiations of the military clauses of Versailles were countered by nothing more ferocious than verbal disapproval. When this clearly did not deter the Führer, each power helped itself as best it could. France did it by hastily concluding a treaty of alliance with the Soviet Union in 1935, and by shoring up its older alliances in southeastern Europe. Great Britain did it by signing a naval agreement with Germany that same year, which permitted parity between the two submarine fleets, but limited the German surface navy to one-third that of Britain's. The wartime partnership between Britain and France seemed long past; each country would have to look after its own interests now.

Against a weaker aggressor, of course, tougher methods might be tried. As Italy invaded Ethiopia, some fifty members of the League of Nations made a bold and novel decision. They formally voted at Geneva to invoke Article 16 of the League Covenant. The article provided for the application of economic sanctions against any member state resorting to force against another, which Italy plainly had. Italy now would face economic strangulation, and have to call off the war.

Italy would do no such thing. Sanctions had been voted, but they were applied in a half-hearted manner only. The Suez Canal was not closed to Italian shipping; thus troops and supplies continued to reach Ethiopia via the shortest available route. Above all, oil was not placed on the embargo list; oil, which of all of Italy's imports was the most crucial.

The West's reasons for this loose interpretation of what sanctions meant were understandable. There was no firm German-Italian alliance yet, and both Britain and France wished to leave Mussolini with some options other than joining up with Hitler. But no matter how defensible the reasons, they ensured that sanctions would fail. And that failure was a blow to the League's remaining power and prestige, from which it would never recover. For the rest of the thirties, the League was no longer even a minor factor in any of Europe's crises. "A debating society," Hitler called it, and he was right.

When Hitler reoccupied the Rhineland in 1936, there was no mention at all of League action, let alone of sanctions. Nor would Britain and France act on their own to oppose him. Perhaps it would all go away if one just forgot about it. A similar three-monkey policy was applied to Spain. While Italians and Germans were pouring into the country to help Franco, and the Russians gave what aid they thought wise in support of the government, the West solemnly maintained the fiction of nonintervention. No volunteers and no supplies must be allowed to reach either side. What this meant, in effect, was that while Franco suffered no acute shortages of supplies, his Republican opponents did, since they were deprived of any official Western aid.

There always remained the weapon of nonrecognition, of course. Let Franco wait before he could receive a British or a French ambassador in full regalia. Let the king of Italy wait even longer before a Western diplomat would address him as Emperor of Ethiopia. And nonrecognition—plus a great deal of editorial indignation—was all that the West found the strength for in response to Hitler's Austrian invasion. But even that sort of reaction would not last long. In the Czech case, as we have seen, the West very actively *helped* Hitler in achieving his objectives. This, then, seemed the end result of Western passivity, of Western appeasement—the craven surrender at Munich. The more brutal of the two dictators, Adolf Hitler, appeared at the height of his triumph.

MOTIVES, EAST AND WEST: THE APPEASERS

Seemed to be? Appeared? The moment has come to look at more than the conventional simplifications about appeasement ("it never works," "you can't give candy to a tiger") and beyond the public arguments of Adolf Hitler ("*Das Diktat von Versailles*," "ten million Germans," "*Das Diktat . . . ,*" "I want no Czechs," ". . . Versailles"). What, instead, were the real, fundamental aims and purposes of both sides?

Let us consider the West first. "Appeasement," wrote one of its severest academic critics, in reality "was free from the overtones the world later acquired. It meant neither cringing nor acting through fear." It meant, instead, that one was acting from a variety of motives—five in particular—that at the time seemed rational and justifiable enough.

The first was the memory of the cost, in resources but above all in lives, of the then very recent World War. The second was that there seemed little reason for pride as one looked at the peace that had ended that war. The third, and related point, was that some at least of the demands that Hitler and Mussolini were raising appeared to have sense and justice on their side. The fourth was the fear of what a new war would mean for Europe. And the fifth, finally, involved the hope, strong especially in Great Britain, that out of the current troubles, disagreements, and dangers might some day evolve a new period of peaceful cooperation.

All these reasons are worth a few more words. As for the cost of the recent war, no pagan sacrifice, nor all the Christian crusades added together, had ever shed a fraction of the blood that was spilled between 1914 and 1918. And to what end had the millions died? They had died, as one of the most incisive of British military historians later put it, in an "expensive audit to prove that the industrial resources of one side were smaller than those of the other."

But had not the audit been worthwhile? Had it not ended in the triumph of the democratic West over the jackbooted Prussians? Had it not, in fact, been unavoidable, since it was forced on Britain and France?

Few people, in the 1920s and 1930s, thought so any more. In 1919, the Allies confidently affirmed, and made the Germans solemnly accept, the so-called war guilt clause—that is to say, "the responsibility of Germany and her allies for causing all the loss and damage . . . of the war imposed on them [i.e. on Britain and France] by the aggression of Germany and her allies." A year later, the British prime minister, David Lloyd George, would say that all governments, the German and his own included, had simply "staggered and stumbled" into war. Mistakes there had been, and no end of them, but guilt was a concept better forgotten. And the historians, as they studied the record of events, tended to agree with Lloyd George rather than with the wartime propagandists to whom none had been responsible for the bloodletting but the Kaiser his henchmen.

Logically, then, the peace settlement came under attack. If Berlin, or Vienna, had been no more culpable than anyone else in 1914, what justification could there be for the punitive clauses of Versailles, or of the Paris peace as a whole? Also, if war were ever to be allowed to come again, the reasons would have to be very much more compelling than in retrospect they appeared to have been in 1914. In the absence of such overwhelming reasons, it was peace, and peace again, that one should be pursuing.

"When I think of those four terrible years," said Britain's prime minister, Neville Chamberlain, to a gathering of his Conservative party followers in the summer of 1938, "and I think of the 7,000,000 of young men who were cut off in their prime, the 13,000,000 who were maimed and mutilated, the misery and the suffering of the mothers and the fathers, the sons and the daughters, and the relatives and the friends of those who were killed, and the wounded, then I am bound to say again what I have said before, and what I say now, not only to you, but to all the world—in war, whichever side may call itself victor, there are no winners, but all are losers. It is those thoughts which have made me feel that it was my prime duty to strain every nerve to avoid a repetition of the Great War in Europe. And I cannot believe that anyone who is not blinded by party prejudice, anyone who thinks what another war would mean, can fail to agree with me and to desire that I should continue my efforts."

To Chamberlain, then, these were entirely proper, sensible, and worthy efforts. And a majority of Englishmen, and Frenchmen, agreed with him. For, and here perhaps is the heart of appeasement, not only did they feel that war was the ultimate evil, but it seemed to them that Hitler and Mussolini had certain justified, or at any rate discussible, grievances. Why should Italy, almost alone among European powers, do so badly in the search for colonies? Why should Germany be saddled forever with the onus of defeat; and were not the Germans entitled to take some interest in the fate of their ethnic kinsmen across their borders? Once these grievances had been met, once Mussolini and Hitler realized that the West stood ready to negotiate the negotiable, Italy and Germany might well be expected to rejoin the community of peaceful, law-abiding nations.

Besides, what was the alternative? "Meeting force with force" was a brave phrase, but what did it mean? It meant the greatest disaster of all—a new 1914. In fact, a new war would lead to even greater slaughter than the last one. And it would leave in its wake a vastly weakened Europe. Everyone would be the loser. Everyone? No, perhaps not, for there might be one exception—the Soviet Union, which would sit out the war. Lenin's dream of 1917 would then come true, a generation later. An exhausted continent would be Sovietized. The situation was indeed grave, the British foreign secretary, Lord Halifax, instructed his ambassador in Berlin early during the Sudeten crisis, but it could not be allowed to "get out of hand, for then the only ones to profit would be the Communists."

Why let them, while the peaceful alternative—a meeting of certain Axis demands, followed by a period of international cooperation—was still feasible? "I believe," wrote one of Chamberlain's friends and counselors in the mid-thirties, "that if we assist Germany to escape from encirclement to a position of balance in Europe, there is a good chance of the twenty-five years peace of which Hitler spoke." And the French, though not quite so euphoric about the possibilities of fruitful coexistence, were willing to go along with the British. They might have more reservations about Germany's ultimate aims, but they were equally horrified by the prospect of another war. Or, differently and less charitably put—the words are those of Paul Reynaud, one of the principal critics of appeasement in France—"the government of the time was happy to find in British resistance [to stopping Axis aggression] a cover for its own faintheartedness."

MOTIVES, EAST AND WEST:
"TO SECURE THE RACIAL COMMUNITY
AND TO ENLARGE IT"—ADOLF HITLER

Was Reynaud being wise after the event? Perhaps. Certainly many people in the West wanted too much. On the one hand, they would have liked to have seen aggression contained, and if that would undermine Hitler's domestic position as well, so much the better. There was, for all the talk about "waves of the future," little love for his ways in Britain or France. On the other hand, a majority of people, leaders and led alike, wished by all means to prevent another war. Both were worthy aims, but they were irreconcilable.

Still, with two of the aggressor nations, with Italy and Japan, appeasement had some real chance of success, and what was one man's faintheartedness was another man's caution, or even statesmanship.

Italy's foreign aims were, to a large extent, old-fashioned and conventional. What fascist Italy wanted was prestige, or, more specifically, land in Africa. This was cruel news to the Ethiopians, and it would require certain adjustments in the European balance of power. But it was not the sort of issue that presented a major threat to European peace. (There is no effort at cynicism here; we are talking about certain facts of European power politics.) And Mussolini, for all his bluster, was a man who was sensitive to counter-pressure and ready to settle for considerably less than he was demanding from the balcony of the *Palazzo Venezia*. Behind the demagogue there was a man with strong inclinations toward respectability. Both were acts, both were sincere—Mussolini, chin stuck out, in his blackshirt; Mussolini, relaxed, in spats and morning suit at some League of Nations meeting. Which one of the two Duces, the neo-Roman conqueror or the aspiring elder statesman, would win out in the end was in no way predestined in the early thirties, and would to a large degree depend on how the West accommodated itself to him. And while his territorial claims might have less than total justice on their side, they were not unprecedented. European diplomacy had had to cope with worse, and without having recourse to general war. They were, in sum, negotiable and hence absorbable demands.

Japan's aims, it was true, were more ambitious than that. Japan was not asking for some minor border rectification, or for delayed recognition as one imperial power among many, and a minor one at that. Japan, instead, wanted to be master of East Asia, wanted, in the words of her own propagandists, to run half a continent as the "Greater East Asia Co-Prosperity Sphere." The phrase lacked the felicity of what Dr. Goebbels' shop was turning out, but it described the Japanese intentions correctly enough. And it contained the threat of years of warfare in Asia. But that was it—of warfare in *Asia*. Japan's aggression might, of course, some day involve the country in conflict with either Russia or the United States, great powers both, but one was only partly a European power, and the other entirely non-European; and the Atlantic still was a very large ocean in the 1930s.

None of this may make the Japanese aims any more just or admirable, though these lines are being written with the benefit of that perspective that the passage of time brings even to the dullest historian, who can note that while the appellation fortunately has changed, the world has been living, quite happily and profitably, with a Japanese-led Greater East Asia Co-Prosperity Sphere for some years now. Nor will it make the Japanese methods of the time—conquest by sword, not by transistor—any more appealing. But the point is that the thirties were still very much a Europe-centered decade, the last for some time to come, but Paris-London-Rome-Berlin-centered nonetheless. It was in Europe that power resided, or was assumed to reside; it was in those capitals that the crucial decisions affecting war and peace were still made.

And it would be over the issue of the unprecedented territorial ambitions that one European power harbored against another, or rather several others, that war would come. It is time, therefore, to take a look at what Hitler's true aims were. We have seen his publicly announced ones—the revision of Versailles and the protection of some ethnic Germans—and they hardly looked that much more threatening than those of Italy or Japan. Had they been all that drove him, appeasement might well have been a reasonable risk, and a policy greatly praised by historians today. But they were not; here, too, the German leader lived in a world apart from his Japanese or Italian allies, whose professed and real aims were just about identical. What Hitler truly wanted was on a grander scale by far than what he told even his party rally audiences.

Hitler's foreign aims, formulated long before he became chancellor, were of two kinds. One was immediate and minimal. The other was long range and maximal. The minimum program provided for the union of the German-speaking Austria created by the victors in 1919 with the German Reich. "German Austria," he had written on the first page of *Mein Kampf*, "must return to the great German mother country, but not for any economic reasons. No and no again. Even if, from an economic perspective, this union were to make no difference; yes, even if it were harmful, it would have to take place nonetheless. *Common blood belongs in a common Reich.* As long as the German people cannot even manage to unite its own sons in a common state, it has no right to colonizing activity. Only when the borders of the Reich include every last German, and the ability to assure his food supply no longer exists, will there arise, from the nation's dire need, the moral right to acquire foreign soil and foreign territory. The plow will then become the sword, and from the tears of war will grow posterity's daily bread."

The long-range program envisaged a German expansion into southeastern and eastern Europe that would provide space for large numbers of German settlers. It was clearly connected with his first aim. *Anschluss* with Austria would be the initial step into southeastern Europe; besides, only after the creation of a Greater Germany would "there arise . . . the moral right to acquire foreign soil." It was also more flexible, however. Just how soon he would move, and with, or against, which power, he was prepared to leave to the conditions and opportunities of the moment. Thus he might, temporarily at least, ally himself with the Poles against the Russians, or with the Russians against the Poles. But what was clear was that in addition to incorporating Austria, he was intent on moving into Czechoslovakia and, ultimately, into European Russia. The great prize of which he dreamed was the wealth of the Ukraine and of the Crimea. What Hitler wanted, and he would say so quite plainly in the beginning, therefore had little to do with "righting the wrongs of Versailles." His intent, rather, as one of the best-informed American historians of the subject put it, was to "seize lands never ruled by the Hohenzollerns. His goal . . . was conquest, not treaty revision."

Or, to quote Hitler's own words, again from *Mein Kampf*: "To demand the borders of 1914 is political nonsense of such a degree and consequence that it appears a crime. . . . The borders of 1914 meant nothing to the German nation. . . . We National Socialists, by contrast, must without wavering keep to our foreign policy aim, which is *to secure to the German nation the soil and space to which it is entitled on this earth. . . .*

"Thus we National Socialists consciously put an end to the foreign policy of our prewar period. We begin again where things ended six centuries ago. We put a stop to the eternal drive of the Teuton to Europe's South and West, and cast our eyes to the land in the East. We finally halt the colonial and economic policies of the prewar period, and move on to the territorial policy of the future.

"But if we speak of new soil and territory in Europe today, we can think primarily only of Russia and of the subject states bordering it."

And again, a few years later, in a sequel to *Mein Kampf* written in 1928, but not published at the time, since some second thoughts suggested the wisdom of not being quite so outspoken about his foreign objectives, he wrote:

"Germany resolves to change to a clear, far-sighted policy of expansion. It shall thus turn away from all attempts at world trade and international industrial enterprise, and instead concentrate all its forces on providing our nation with sufficient living space—and thus with a way of life as well—for the next hundred years. Since such space can lie only in the east, the needs of being a naval power recede into the background. It is by means of building a major land power that Germany shall try once again to battle for its interests."

Did Hitler mean to use that land power, did his aims entail the risk of war? He himself gave the answer, and it was an unapologetic yes. The goals he had in mind, he said in *Mein Kampf*, "before God and German generations to come, will justify an investment of blood. Before God, since we have been placed in this world destined to engage in an eternal struggle for our daily bread, as creatures who will not receive anything for nothing, and who owe their positions as lords of the earth only to their genius and to the courage with which they will fight for and defend it; before German generations to come, since we will have spilled no citizen's blood which will not allow a thousand others to live in the future. The soil, on which in times to come generations of German farmers will be able to procreate strong sons, will sanction risking the lives of the sons of today and will, in future ages, absolve the statesmen responsible—even if the present generation should persecute them —of blood guilt and national sacrifice."

Besides, it would be a relatively small investment in blood. Hitler had no desire for universal war. What he had in mind was a limited war, was a campaign or series of campaigns in the East only. Hitler was not suicidal. Exotic though his aims might be, his methods of pursuing them were perfectly rational. He had not the least desire to fight the British, for instance. On the contrary, he wanted England for an ally as much as he wanted Italy. The British, after all, were racially sound, nor was there, in his view, any cause for Anglo-German friction, since British energies and interests were directed at their overseas empire, while his were centered on continental expansion. The Italians, while less desirably Nordic, had shown their worth by opting for fascism. Besides, he clearly needed Italy's cooperation, or at least Italy's toleration, if he were to take Austria. So, in his way, he was perfectly sincere in his protestations of friendship for both countries. Nor did he particularly wish to march against what he and many others considered the West's weakest power, France. If the opportunity presented itself, if France should come close to internal collapse, he might move in for the *coup de grâce*, but even in such an eventuality, as he said in *Mein Kampf*, it would have to be "basic that Germany truly see the destruction of France as a means to an end, which is to enable our nation subsequently to expand elsewhere at long last."

To "expand elsewhere," but why? Because, and the phrase is as characteristic of Hitler as any, all mankind was involved in "an eternal struggle." The conquest of new territory, the struggle of the strong against the weak, the fit against the less fit was profitable, yes, and useful, for "every healthy, unspoiled nation." But it was more, too—it was "something natural" and beneficial to all mankind. "He who would ban this sort of contention from earth for all eternity might possibly do away with the struggle of man against man, but he would also do away with earth's highest force for evolution."

Means and ends, in a way very real to Hitler, were in perfect harmony. For it was Hitler's interpretation of Social Darwinism that shaped his foreign as well as his domestic policies. He saw life as a constant struggle among nations, races, and social groups as much as between species. The deepest meaning of life, in every one of its aspects, lay in the evolution that accompanied the survival of the fittest. Let the Germans, their Aryan purity and health restored by the removal of the Jews, prove their superior fitness over the Slavs now; let the Russian wastelands bloom under the management of racially superior German engineers and equally superior German farmers. It would take a bloody war to bring them there, and that was cruel. But what was not? And consider the prize: the expansion of German strength, and the eastward spread of civilization, of civilization brought by the fitter, and only true creator of culture, the Aryan. "If we were to divide mankind into three species: the culture-creators, the culture-bearers and the culture-destroyers, only the Aryan would be likely to fit the first definition. It is to him that we must trace the foundations and the walls of all that human beings have created."

But were not all these the fantasies of youthful, irresponsible

Hitler? True, his campaign against the Jews ("the most powerful antipode to the Aryan is the Jew"), and others considered undesirable or unfit, tended to show that he had not abandoned the domestic part of his program. But he was chancellor of a great nation now, not just the leader of a radical party given to certain ideological eccentricities. The Hitler of the Storm and Stress period was one person, might not another, more sober Hitler, emerge now that he held power and responsibility? Had he not, in fact, given some sensible and conciliatory foreign policy speeches since assuming office—calling for international understanding, advocating disarmament, and offering nonaggression treaties to just about any country that was at all interested in signing one? Where was the Hitler speech given after 1933 in which there was so much as a hint that he meant to take Prague, or open up the Ukraine to German colonization?

The answer was that there was none—or rather, no public one. For in private, to his close associates, Hitler made it clear beyond a doubt that his original aims dominated his thinking as much as ever, and what was more, that he was ready now to translate them into reality. Two confidential speeches in particular illustrate this as much as anything. One was given to a small audience of his chief aides, the other to a larger one, consisting of Germany's leading newspaper editors.

Early in November 1937, Hitler summoned a group of five ranking military and civilian leaders to the Chancellery in Berlin. Present were the foreign minister and the minister of war, and the commanders-in-chief of the army, navy, and air force. Present, too, was Hitler's military aide, Colonel Friedrich Hossbach, who took notes during the meeting, and afterwards wrote a detailed summing up of what had been said. (Hence, what transpired at the conference is often referred to as the Hossbach Protocol, or even the Hossbach meeting, though it was very much the Führer's, and not the colonel's.)

He wished to speak, said Hitler, about Germany's objectives in the world, and what he now had to say on that topic was of such basic importance that he wanted it to be regarded, "in the event of his death, as his last will and testament."

The aim of his policy, Hitler went on, was to "secure and preserve the racial community and to enlarge it," and the only way that was possible was by continental expansion, was, more specifically, by moving east. Consider the alternatives, he said. It had been suggested that Germany might secure her greatness and her survival by more peaceable means—by a spectacular increase in industrial production, or by a greater share of world trade, or by the recovery of some of the colonies lost in 1919. None of these answers made any real sense, said Hitler. As for the first, Germany could never be truly self-sufficient within her present borders, no matter what the industrial growth rate. As for the second, "opportunities for economic expansion, for countries outside of the great economic empires, were severely limited." Besides, to depend for survival on foreign trade meant "military weakness." As for the third, finally, it was utopian to expect the British to return any of Germany's colonies if only "because of the opposition of the Dominions." (The argument he had made in *Mein Kampf* had been more direct. African or Asian colonies, he had written, were a source of weakness; too much racial strength was dissipated if the home base were small and the dominion over colonial areas large.)

His conclusion, said Hitler, was that there remained only one way to solve "the question of space," and that was by expansion. The "space necessary . . . can only be sought in Europe, not, as in the liberal-capitalist view, in the exploitation of colonies. It is not a matter of acquiring population, but of gaining space for agricultural use. Moreover, areas producing raw materials can more usefully be sought in Europe, in immediate proximity to the Reich, than overseas." Just where in Europe? Where he had said in *Mein Kampf*—toward the east, with the first moves to be those against Austria and Czechoslovakia. By what means? By force of arms, as he had predicted in *Mein Kampf.*

"Germany's problems," he said for the benefit of the slow learners among his audience, "could be solved only by means of force, and that was never without its attendant risks." But other German statesmen had taken such risks, and won. "The campaigns of Frederick the Great for Silesia, and Bismarck's wars against Austria and France had involved unheard-of risk," but the speed and efficiency of the action had kept the wars limited and the gains high.

This left, then, the question of when to strike and how. He was, he said, with one exception flexible on both. If France's internal situation, for instance, should suddenly deteriorate to such a degree that the French army "was incapable of use for war against

Germany," then, "the time for action against the Czechs" would come very quickly, while the Austrian move might wait. If France, on the other hand, should show some readiness to fight, then Germany must "overthrow Czechoslovakia and Austria simultaneously, in order to protect the threat to our flank in any possible operation against the West." But he doubted that any such western campaign would really be called for, since he felt that Britain and France "had already tacitly written off the Czechs." So, he thought, had the Poles and the Russians, and even if not, it was likely that a quick German victory would frighten them into immobility.

But while he was thus ready for a fair amount of improvisation, there was one exception. He was unwilling, he said, to wait with unlimited patience before acting. He had set himself a time limit, and was resolved to strike in six to eight years at the very most. He was getting older, he explained, and if he waited any longer than that both the strength of the German armed forces and of the Nazi movement would lose their momentum. It hence was his "unalterable decision to solve Germany's problem of space at the latest by 1943–45, though if circumstances were favorable before that, he would of course strike sooner."

An animated discussion followed Hitler's statements. This, after all, was a high-level policy conference, and not a party rally where nothing but *Heils* were allowed the audience. Germany's military preparedness was not quite at the stage where the Führer thought it to be, suggested the army's commander-in-chief, and was backed by his minister. The diplomatic constellation was perhaps a bit less favorable, too, said the foreign minister. None of them assailed the Führer's ideas directly; they had all learned what a high official at the foreign ministry after the war would put into words, which was that in arguing with the deranged it was wise to bring up points that were likely to appeal to the deranged. Hence the arguments they used were pragmatic, not ideological, let alone moral. Still, their opposition to the proposed moves was plain enough.

Hitler heard them out patiently, responded with no apparent anger, and within five months had all of them, under one pretext or another, removed from their positions. (Manufactured charges of homosexuality forced the commander-in-chief into retirement. The foreign minister, more circumspectly, was elevated to the newly created position of president of a secret cabinet council that was so secret that it never met, and was replaced by the entirely pliable

Joachim von Ribbentrop. Police files about the indeed scandalous past of the woman the minister of war had recently married were made available to the army's top echelons, and it was Hitler himself who took over the war ministry when that affair was over.)

But then, the conference and its aftermath had taken place before what many people, then and now, considered his greatest triumph, before Munich. Did not the world deal with a happier, satiated Hitler after 1938? His specific references had been to Austria and Czechoslovakia at the meeting Colonel Hossbach had recorded, and he was now complete master over one—Austria—and victor over the other. For what remained of the Czech state was obviously dependent on his good will for survival. Might not a new phase, of consolidation and reason, be inaugurated after 1938, as it had been under Bismarck after 1871, when the nation had achieved its major aims of that period?

The clearest answer, once again, was provided by Hitler himself. Six weeks after Munich, on November 10, 1938, Hitler summoned several hundred leading German newspaper editors and publishers to Berlin to listen to his ideas about the road ahead. There was no subsequent discussion this time. On the contrary, there was a reference to the possible need to "exterminate" skeptics, which had a certain sobering effect upon his audience.

It was a long and rambling speech, whose gist, however, was perfectly plain: The German press must prepare the public for further foreign moves on Hitler's part. The press had supported him well in the past; it must be prepared to do so again. In fact, it might have supported him a bit *too* well, he suggested, since his assurances of peace had fooled the Germans, for whom they had not been meant, as well as foreigners, for whom they had been. Would his audience please understand that it was necessity, and not conviction, that had made him play the advocate of nonviolence.

"Circumstances have forced me to talk for decades about practically nothing but peace. Only by constantly stressing Germany's desire for peace, by dwelling on her peaceful intentions, could I, step by step, gain freedom for the German people. Only thus could I provide it with the arms that in each case were essential before the next step could be taken. It is natural that such peace propaganda, undertaken for decades, has its worrisome aspects too. For the result might easily be that the idea would take hold in many people's heads that the present government was by definition identical with the will and the decision to maintain peace under all circumstances. But that would not only lead to a wrong evaluation of this system. Above all, it would, instead of armoring the German people against coming events, fill it with a spirit of defeatism, which in the long run could not but deprive this regime of its successes. The reason that for years I talked about nothing but peace was that I had to."

But now the next stage was at hand. The press would have to prepare the ground for new achievements, "to strengthen, step by step, the self-confidence of the German people." There would be cowards and weaklings predicting failure and doom—he was used to them, and he had proved all of them wrong in the past. So he would again in the future, if only the press would play up "the strength of the nation that has been proven over the centuries and will ever remain." The nation must be made to understand that Hitler would achieve for it the same miracle he had for the party—the creation, from the smallest of beginnings, of a vast and powerful organization. Germany "must learn a *fanatic* belief in final victory." And why should it not? Just because the faint of heart were counseling caution? He had heard those people "who said, 'Isn't the Führer dealing in phantasies? Does he really believe in those possibilities?'" To which his answer was that he did. There was no nation as strong as National Socialist Germany—that was the point the press must hammer home. "I am of the conviction today that our nation, in its gradual racial improvement, represents the highest value that exists on this earth at this time. Always think of this when you consider statistics. Yes, the United States has a population of 126 or 127 million. But if you deduct the Germans, the Irish, the Negroes, the Jews, etc., and all the others, there remain not even 60 million Anglo-Saxons, people who consider themselves Anglo-Saxons. The British Empire possesses fewer than 46 million Britishers on its home soil. The French 'Empire' does not even have 37 million real Frenchmen. Italy has over 40 million Italians. Poland has only 17 million Poles left. *But*: in Germany, as of 1940, we will have *80 million people of one race*, and around us another 8 million who in a racial sense really belong to us. He who doubts the future of this huge human block, he who does not believe in this future, merely shows that he is a weakling. I believe in this future *unconditionally*. We once *were* the greatest of Empires. Then we got tired and exhausted, wasted our strength in a process of internal dissolution, and became a small power. Now, after a crisis of 400, 300 years, our nation is in a period of regeneration. And I know very well: we now stand at the beginning of our German life and thus our German future. To prepare this future, to help shape it, so that the future will become real, must be the greatest happiness for all of us."

YEAR OF DISASTER: 1939

IN THE CASTLE OF BOHEMIA'S KINGS: MUNICH TO PRAGUE

Munich, then—and this is essential to an understanding both of the nature of appeasement and of the origins of World War II—to Hitler had not been a triumph of his cunning at all, had not been the end of the chapter of Nazi expansion. What he had wanted that fall was not some Sudeten Germans but Prague, and he had been entirely ready to fight a small war in the East for it. In fact, he had been looking forward to it. "That fellow," he complained to his entourage about Neville Chamberlain after Munich, "has spoiled my entry into Prague."

Why had he allowed him to do so? Because there had been pressure from his Axis partner to agree to a peaceful settlement; Mussolini felt, and rightly so, that Italy was unprepared for a major European war. (It was an attitude typical of Mussolini. He enjoyed winning as much as the next man, but he was ready to drop out of the game when the stakes got too high.) And what was even more important, Hitler sensed that psychologically, Germany, too, was not yet ready for war. He had indeed played the role of peacelover too long and too well. One incident above all others demonstrated this to him during the Sudeten crisis. It took place a few days before the Big Four met at Munich.

To put some pressure on his conference partners, and to arouse the enthusiasm of his own people, Hitler ordered an entire motorized division, supplied with live ammunition and ready for battle, to parade through Berlin. Let it drive past the British embassy, let the Berliners see the force he had built. The route would end at the Chancellery, where Hitler, from his balcony, would salute the division.

Such things had been stage-managed before, and successfully so. But not this time. People fell silent as they saw the tanks roll by. This was real. This was 1914 all over again. Even in front of the Chancellery, there were no *Heils*. Hitler, watching, stepped back from his balcony into the room behind it. "He gave orders to have the lights turned out," a foreign ministry official who was with him recalled. "He then placed himself behind the curtains and watched the scene for quite a while. Suddenly he turned around and said, harshly, 'With a people like that I cannot make war yet.'"

The impression was confirmed at Munich, when the frenetic applause that Chamberlain and Daladier received from the assembled crowds was correctly interpreted by Hitler as a demonstration for peace. But people's minds could be changed; "not *yet*," he had said. Hence the speech to the press; hence a resumption of the public campaign against the Czechs within weeks after Munich. ("Czechs continue to oppress . . ." "German interests threatened . . .") Hence, too, secret orders to prepare the next move east. It would finish the job left uncompleted at Munich and stimulate the public's appetite for further gains. The plan, now that the Sudeten pretext was gone, was this: Germany would establish direct control over the Czech part, or Bohemia and Moravia, as he called it in his directives, using the old Habsburg term for the area. Slovakia, on the other hand, might have some nominal independence, though in fact it would have to rely on Germany for its survival.

Ten days after Chamberlain had returned to London proclaiming "peace for our time," Hitler sent a brief inquiry to the chief of the army's high command, General Keitel: How long would it take, and what measures would be required, "to break all Czech resistance in Bohemia and Moravia?" No particular difficulties, replied Keitel, and he knew what he was talking about, for Munich had deprived Czechoslovakia not only of its Germans but also of its strategic border area. Thus assured, Hitler instructed the armed forces to prepare "the liquidation of Czechoslovakia." The date was October 21; Chamberlain's forecast now was three weeks old.

In the spring of 1939, everything was ready. "Our patience was exhausted," Hitler's foreign minister, Joachim von Ribbentrop, told the Italian ambassador in Berlin on March 14. "An attempt has been made to make Czechia a pawn once more in the European game. The Führer intends to lance the abscess." He would do so with a sharp and quick knife. As Ribbentrop was speaking, the Czech president, Emil Hacha, was summoned to Germany. He was told by Hitler that post-Munich Czechoslovakia seemed to have learned nothing from its sins, that he, the Führer, would tolerate this no longer and had decided on the state's "incorporation into the German Reich." The Czechs could, of course, fight. But in that case, the German air force would obliterate Prague—here Göring was called in to supply details—while the German army would break any resistance on the ground "with brute force." So let Hacha provide "the last good turn he could render the Czech people" and *request* German protection, in which case the Czechs might receive some "autonomy and a certain measure of national freedom."

After a grueling night session during which the Czech president fainted once and had to be revived by Hitler's physician, Hacha gave in, signing a document (prepared by the Germans) in which he placed "with entire confidence the destiny of the Czech people and the Czech land in the hands of the Führer of the German Reich."

On the following morning, on March 15, German troops marched into Prague. They met with no resistance, and in the evening, Hitler followed them into the capital. Here was his triumphal entry after all. "Czechia," he proclaimed from Hradcany Castle, the ancient seat of Bohemia's kings, had ceased to exist. Slovakia would have its nominal independence, the Czech part not even that, but would become, instead, the German "Protectorate of Bohemia and Moravia."

It was Hitler's most fateful decision since he had become chancellor. Gone now was the pretense that he wanted nothing but to revise Versailles or to protect Germans abroad. This was Slavic territory, not German. Nor had the Czech lands at any time belonged to the pre-1919 Reich.

"MILITARISM IN ACTION": PRAGUE TO WAR

How would the West react? With temporary annoyance, thought Hitler, but without the strength or will to act. "I knew it," he said during his Prague stay when he was told that neither Britain nor France were mobilizing. "A couple of weeks from now, no one will be talking about it any more."

Too much optimism. "Please inform German Government," the British foreign secretary instructed his ambassador in Berlin, "that His Majesty's Government desire to make it plain to them that they cannot but regard the events of the past few days as a complete repudiation of the Munich agreement and a denial of the spirit in which the negotiatiors of that agreement bound themselves to co-operate for a peaceful settlement."

This was the break. Appeasement was dead. "A New Dawn," had been the London *Times* lead editorial after Munich. After Prague, it was "Militarism in Action."

In a way, what followed Prague was anticlimactic. Against a Hitler who seemed to have justice on his side the West would not act; against this Hitler, it felt it had to. And he already seemed to have chosen his next victim—Poland. Soon after Prague, a German press campaign against that country got under way. The list of grievances was being aired: the Poles were mistreating their German minority; the Poles were proving obdurate in their dealings with Germany. Poland, at Versailles, had received a "corridor" through German territory to give it access to the sea. Some changes were overdue here, suggested the Nazi press, yet the Poles seemed struck with blindness when faced with the problem. And they were equally stubborn about any change in status for Danzig—a town German in population, yet established by the victors as a free city in 1919 to provide Poland with a seaport.

It was, the western powers felt, the Czech story all over again. Limited grievances were being used as a cover for unlimited ambitions. Or, as one writer on the period put it, "The Germans had, as they had with Czechoslovakia, legitimate grounds for complaint. The Poles had legitimate grounds for anxiety."

This time, however, the West reacted differently. In case of any action threatening Polish independence, Chamberlain declared on March 31, 1939, in which "the Polish government accordingly considered it vital to resist with their national forces, His Majesty's Government would feel themselves bound at once to lend the Polish government all the support in their power."

It was a unilateral British guarantee of Poland. And although, strictly speaking, no similar promise on the part of France was needed, since there already existed a Franco-Polish defense treaty, Chamberlain added that he was authorized by the French to say that they were joining in this guarantee of Poland's independence.

Britain's decision produced an oddly wavering mood in Hitler. On the one hand, he did very much want to move against Poland next. Western suspicions had been correct enough here. Two weeks after Prague, he ordered the necessary military plans prepared, setting September 1 as the deadline for action. On the other hand, he dreaded the idea of a general war. And the one country above all that he still did not want as an enemy was Great Britain.

Perhaps, he told himself, Chamberlain had not really been in earnest when he made the British promise to Warsaw. Or if he had, perhaps his mind could still be changed by some exceedingly clever diplomatic move. And by the end of the summer, Hitler indeed produced if not his cleverest, then certainly his most astounding, move of all—a pact with the Soviet Union.

On August 23, 1939, there was signed in Moscow, between the two nations that had until then, in Stalin's delicate phrase, "poured buckets of slop over each other," a treaty of friendship and nonaggression. Or rather, that was the public part. For it also contained a secret addendum, which provided for the division of Poland (with the country's eastern half going to Russia, and the western half to Germany), and for the establishment of spheres of influence elsewhere, with Finland, Estonia, Latvia, and the Bessarabian part of Rumania to fall into the Russian sphere, and Lithuania into the German.

How could one account for this treaty, startling even in an age and among powers not noted for their general probity? On Stalin's side, there were several motives—his resentment over having been excluded from the Munich conference, his old and persistent suspicions of the West, his awareness of Russia's military weakness (the great purges, which had spread to the armed forces, were only a year or two in the past), his hope that, to his ultimate gain, he might act the onlooker in a war between Hitler and the West. Above all, however, it was the Polish and the Baltic prizes that tempted him. Here, at long last, was the chance to restore Russia's tsarist borders.

On the German side, the motives were less mixed. Hitler wanted war against Poland, and if, to have his back free for that war, he had to reach a temporary understanding with an enemy of nazism—bolshevism—as old and supposedly unalterable as the Jews, so he would. What good, he argued, was the Franco-British guarantee of Poland when the facts of European geography precluded any direct military aid? Now that the Czechs were in his power, only the Russians could help the Poles. There were, as he knew, some half-hearted attempts on the part of London and Paris that summer to obtain promises of such assistance from Russia, but two factors made their failure all but inevitable. One was the deep suspicion that existed between London and Moscow. Chamberlain might no longer trust Hitler, but he still had the same reservations he always had about an accommodation with Russia. They were feelings that were reciprocated in full by Stalin. The other was that the Poles were unwilling to be aided by their Soviet neighbors. How, they asked—and subsequent events were to show how intelligent the question had been—were they ever to get rid of their liberators later?

This, then, was the situation in which Hitler made his about-face, pledging friendship and eastern Poland to Stalin. The pact, he calculated, would deprive the Poles of their only possible source of aid, that of Russia, making the Western powers' pledge of assistance an academic affair. London and Paris must surely see this, which meant that after some suitable verbal protests they could be expected to forget, more or less graciously, about their guarantee to Poland.

Did Hitler mean the pledge to Stalin to last forever? Of course not. But it would serve to neutralize the Soviets as well as the democracies for the moment. It had always been part of his genius, after all, to take on his enemies one by one. Thus he had assured the Czechs of his peaceful intentions during the *Anschluss*. Thus he had let the Poles take a slice of Czech territory during the Sudeten crisis. He would turn on Stalin again when the time came. But right now was the time to turn on Warsaw.

So he did, as Stalin knew he would. "Both sides," wrote George Kennan in his account of Soviet foreign policy, "in signing the pact, were aware that it sealed the fate of Poland, that war—a German-Polish war, that is—would be only a matter of days."

WAR

One week after the pact's signing in Moscow, on August 30, 1939, Hitler ordered the German armed forces to begin the attack on Poland. Here it was, his small war.

Only it wasn't. For the first time, one of Hitler's major diplomatic calculations went wrong.

On September 3, after a demand that German troops be withdrawn from Poland had gone unanswered, Great Britain declared war on Germany. So did France; the Polish guarantee was being honored by both. World War II had begun.

A witness remembered the scene in the Reich Chancellery that day. "A disconcerted Hitler brought out the words, 'So they did declare war after all.' After a short silence, he got hold of himself again. 'Even if they declared war on us to meet their supposed alliance obligations, it does not necessarily follow that they will actually fight.' Ribbentrop, as was his custom, agreed vocally." In another room, out of the Führer's hearing, a very sober Göring said, "if we lose this war, may heaven protect us."

Within two years, the war had become global in scope, as first the Soviet Union and then the United States were drawn into it. The involvement of one had been very much planned by Hitler. That of the other he had dreaded, and tried to avoid as best he could.

War with the Soviet Union had long been one of his aims, of course, and the time to realize it seemed to him to have come in 1941. The Polish campaign had been even easier than he or his high command had anticipated. Six weeks had been enough to smash the Polish army and force the country into surrender. There had followed, in 1940, an almost equally lightning campaign against France—by way of Belgium *and* Holland this time—a Schlieffen Plan that worked. Only the British were still in the war; even so, he felt secure in the West. The moment had come to seize the opportunity he had described in *Mein Kampf* seventeen years earlier—the moment to seek space for German colonizers in a Russia that, as he saw it, had been weakened beyond repair by Jews and bolsheviks. "The huge empire in the East is ready to collapse," he had predicted in *Mein Kampf,* and the intervening years had brought no change either in his aims or in his estimate of communist Russia's strength. "We only have to kick in the door," he told one of his generals as the invasion of Russia was being prepared, "and the whole rotten structure will come crashing down."

That it did not was the second of his great miscalculations, as fateful in its way as the first, as the illusion that Britain had been bluffing. The third was to come later in 1941, as the United States, by way of the Japanese attack on Pearl Harbor, entered the war. He had very much hoped to be able to keep Washington out of the conflict. Visions of World War I, and of the role America had played then, were haunting him. In consequence, he reacted very coolly to a number of clearly unneutral American acts after 1939. This was a very rational Hitler who would not be provoked.

American opinion, he knew, was at least partly on his side. It was not that many Americans wished him well. But a great many did wish to stay out of the conflict. America's participation in the first world war had brought the country no thanks and the world no peace; let America therefore remain neutral in the second.

Yet in Franklin Roosevelt, Hitler had an opponent as determined, and as crafty, as he was. Roosevelt was no American Chamberlain. Sacrificing Europe to Hitler, he felt, would no more appease the dictator than handing him the Sudeten area had. Besides, even if Hitler's further territorial ambitions might conceivably be curbed, Nazi rule simply was too indecent to be allowed to prevail. America's fate and the fate of Britain and the Continent were linked by bonds of common history and of common interest. If Europe were Hitler's, America would no longer be truly free.

Hence, despite the country's isolationist mood, and despite the risk of German retaliation, Roosevelt took a number of measures to aid the Allies that, had Hitler wished it, would have provided him with a far more valid excuse for war than the hapless Poles ever had. Thus in the fall of 1940, the United States transferred fifty supposedly "over-age" destroyers to Britain in exchange for the lease of naval bases in the Atlantic. Thus, half a year later, the United States, under the Lend-Lease Act, began the massive shipment of arms and supplies to Great Britain. Thus, in the fall of 1941, Roosevelt, as commander-in-chief, gave orders to the American navy to destroy Axis submarines on sight.

Still, Hitler, while privately furious at Roosevelt (it was plain, he told his intimates, that the President had Jewish blood), would not allow himself to be drawn into a confrontation with the United States. Time after time, his response to provocation was forbearance. What in the end changed this pattern were events occurring in an area beyond Hitler's control, in the Far East. The Germans, since the mid-thirties, had certain commitments to the Japanese, which had been formalized, in 1940 in the Tripartite pact among Germany, Italy, and Japan. The Japanese had been taking advantage of the war in Europe to advance their campaign of conquest in Asia, which had begun with their invasion of Manchuria in 1931. Thus, with France defeated, they pushed into Indo-China; thus, with Britain's energies taken up in the fight with Hitler, they speeded up their conquest of mainland China. Hitler clearly saw the risks that this policy entailed. In several conversations, he tried to deflect the Japanese from any action that might involve them in a collision with the United States, urging them, instead, to attack Britain's holdings in Asia, telling them how easy and profitable it might be, for instance, to take Singapore. But the Japanese were aware of the fact that the one power—now that Britain was weak and France occupied—that could successfully oppose their scheme for East Asia was the United States. And on December 7, 1941, Japanese aircraft, without warning (and without any prior consultation among the members of the Tripartite pact) struck at the United States naval base at Pearl Harbor. Within the space of two hours, five battleships and three cruisers had been sunk, 150 aircraft destroyed, and some 2,000 people killed. Something else, too had been killed, however. It was the debate between isolationists and interventionists in the United States. The day after Pearl Harbor, Congress, by an overwhelming majority, declared war on Japan.

Nominally, this still left the United States at peace with the Axis. But Hitler no longer was willing to continue his policy of restraint. When he heard the news about Pearl Harbor, he was, as someone close to him put it, "delighted," and on December 11, both Germany and Italy honored their treaty obligations under the Tripartite Pact and declared war on the United States. After all, the war in the West was practically over; in the East, the Russians were in full retreat; and in the Pacific, the Japanese had all but crippled the naval power of the United States. He would win against the world now.

That he would not, we know. But we know, too, how close he

came—victor from Egypt to the Caucasus. In the West, France was his, and Belgium and Holland; in the North, Denmark and Norway; in the Southeast, Yugoslavia and Greece; in the East, Poland and much of European Russia. The appetite was growing with the winning; "the intoxication of a new Alexandrian campaign" was his now too. "Strategic necessity" has always been a powerful stimulant to ambition, of course, but even in the beginning, the desire for conquest in the East had not necessarily precluded the possibility of conquest elsewhere. Albert Speer, his friend and architect who designed the triumphal avenues and buildings planned for a great postwar Berlin, recalled an incident that took place in the summer of 1939. The largest of the monumental buildings was to be a dome structure nearly 1,000 feet in height, which meant that its light opening alone could have held the entire dome of St. Peter's in Rome. The structure was to be topped, as many of the Nazi buildings were, by an eagle holding the swastika. Hitler pointed at the drawing and said: "Let's change that. We don't want the eagle over the swastika here; we'll have him ruling over a globe here."

Building and eagle remained on the drawing board, yet for several years the Continent was Hitler's. The tide would not turn until 1942 or 1943, and even after that he would fight on to the bitter end, to more death and suicide. It would take six years in all to defeat him, and casualties unheard of in history. The statistics record about 30 million deaths in World War II, half of them civilian. This was nearly three times the number killed in World War I—and that war had claimed twice as many victims as had all the wars during the two centuries preceding 1914.

Yet there was, after 1945, rather less discussion over whether it had been worth it than after 1918. It was too easy to imagine a world turned Nazi. Besides, there were, when all was said and done, even fewer alternatives in 1939 than in 1914.

PART 2

DOCUMENTS

CHAPTER ONE

The Great War and After

RECOLLECTIONS

Only twenty-one years passed between the end of the first World War and the beginning of the second, a shorter period, by far, than that which separates us from the end of World War II. The mood of the 1930s, hence, was determined to a very large degree by what had occurred between 1914 and 1919. One thing that had—the most crucial, perhaps—was that these years had shown how utterly brutal modern war could be. Nearly all participants had entered the war with unquestioning patriotism, even with enthusiasm; many were to quit it in horror. One Frenchman's account may stand for many. It is that of René Naegelen, a twenty-year-old French army sergeant in 1914, who would later become a socialist deputy, and, for all his memories of battle, an active member of the French resistance against the Nazis in World War II.

September 24, 1915. On the eve of the great Champagne offensive, my regiment in parade order listened to the intoxicating words delivered to the troops on that day by the commander in chief. The brass instruments and the cymbals gave the tone. The colonel's voice carried well: "Soldiers of the Republic: The hour has come to attack and to win. In the wake of a hurricane of iron and fire, you will storm forward together! Your onslaught won't be resisted. Its first wave will carry you to the enemy's batteries, behind the fortified area from which they are opposing us. You will fight them relentlessly until victory is yours. Fight wholeheartedly for the liberation of your country, for the triumph of Justice and Liberty!"

On that day—however incredible it may seem—I would not have changed places with anyone, not even for an empire!

We advanced only 4 miles, sustaining heavy losses, then digging trenches into the chalky soil of Champagne, burrowing our way into the ground during the long months of a dismally trying war.

February, 1916. Verdun! The Kaiser's Germany also hoped for the end of the conflict. Verdun! The famous battle was to last six months, without achieving any other result than the deaths of 370,000 men, Germans and French together.

"Stand your ground!" was General Pétain's order. "No retreat! Meet death on the field! Let survivors launch counterattacks!"

Source: George A. Panichas, ed., *Promise of Greatness, The War of 1914–1918* (John Day, New York, 1968), pp. 169–170.

Having been lost, recaptured, and lost again—sixteen times in the case of a village called Fleury—our positions ultimately remained in the enemy's hands; the breakthrough did not take place.

In June, 1916, my regiment went up to Verdun.

The front line lay ahead of us, concentric and incandescent, its thousands of artillery batteries belching out fire.

That night believers and unbelievers alike prayed to God, "Lord, let me come back. I am not guilty. Protect me!"

Were they already marked, the men who were to lie in that charnel house? Would I ever say, "I was at Verdun," or would others say of me, "He was killed at Verdun"?

All loaded up and harnessed like pack mules, we set out at dusk in order to reach the front line before daybreak, stumbling in the shell holes, panting, running, stamping, harassedly ducking under the blasts of explosions. The night seemed to proceed toward some monstrous collective crime.

May I tell you my most horrible experience? We were facing the famous Fort de Vaux. Dawn laid bare the harrowed ground. The stench of half-putrescent corpses in the process of being shredded by shells made the air fouler still. Overcoat sleeves flapped in the air. A mass of flaccid flesh fell on me; I used my entrenching tool to throw away this remnant of a soldier which stained my uniform.

Three of us were crouching in a hole under the barrage of artillery fire. Then a flame, a blast; then darkness and smoke, the acrid smell of gunpowder. Was I killed or wounded? I cautiously moved my arms and legs. Nothing. My two friends, however, lying one upon the other, were bleeding. The bowels of one were oozing out. The other had a broken leg; there was a red spot spreading on his breast, and he was rolling his panic-stricken eyes. He looked at me silently, imploringly; then unconsciously he unbuttoned his trousers and died urinating upon the gaping wound of his comrade.

Horrified, I fled from their unbearable presence. I looked for shelter, any shelter from the gunfire. But the dead filled all the available craters and drove me away: yesterday's corpses with their features contorted in painful agony or composed after a merciful end, swollen, gray corpses, corpses almost liquefied and alive with worms and flies.

Ten days of deadly thirst in the blazing June sunshine.

Such was the battlefield at Verdun.

PEACEMAKING 1919

If the peace that followed the slaughter had taken account of the new feelings and the new forces that the war had released, if it had been one of justice and of imagination, much might have been forgotten and forgiven. But the Treaty of Paris was an old-fashioned victor's peace ("it would be foolish," said Clemenceau to Wilson, "to treat the Germans with justice") or rather, it was a compromise. It was a compromise between the desire, on the one hand, to prevent another war, and on the other, to punish the losers. Both motives were as understandable as they were irreconcilable. But that was part of the problem only. Another was that more was involved than the fate of the war's best-hated enemy, the Germans. If that had been all, the treaty, while lacking great moral force, might still have been a workable one. But the peace-makers also set about destroying the two great empires that had been on the losing side, Austria-Hungary and Turkey. And they sometimes did so rather casually. Sir Harold Nicolson (1886–1968), a member of the British delegation in Paris, remembered:

May 8, Thursday. Another cloudless day. . . . During the afternoon, there is the first revision of the frontiers of Austria. Go round to the Rue Nitot at luncheon and coach A. J. B[alfour].[1] Down with him to the Quai d'Orsay. There (in that heavy tapestried room, under the simper of Marie de Medicis, with the windows open upon the garden and the sound of water sprinkling from a fountain and from a lawn-hose)—the fate of the Austro-Hungarian Empire is finally settled. Hungary is partitioned by these five distinguished gentlemen—indolently, irresponsibly partitioned—while the water sprinkles on the lilac outside—while the experts watch anxiously—while A.J.B., in the intervals of dialectics on secondary points, relapses into somnolence—while Lansing draws hobgoblins upon his writing pad—while Pichon crouching in his large chair blinks owlishly as decision after decision is actually recorded—while Sonnino, returned to Canossa, is ruggedly polite—while Makino, inscrutable and inarticulate, observes, observes, observes.

They begin with Transylvania, and after some insults flung like tennis balls between Tardieu and Lansing, Hungary loses her South. Then Czecho-Slovakia, and while the flies drone in and out

---

Source: Harold Nicolson, *Peacemaking 1919* (Harcourt, Brace, and Company, New York, 1939), pp. 328–329 (by permission of Harcourt, Brace & World).

[1] Britain's foreign secretary.

of the open windows Hungary loses her North and East. Then the
frontier with Austria, which is maintained intact. Then the
Jugo-Slav frontier, where the Committee's report is adopted
without change. Then tea and macaroons.

Bob Vansittart's play in the evening.

Unfair and illogical treaty.
Punish losers - Ger, Aus.-Hung., Tur.
Prevent another war.

3.   JOHN MAYNARD KEYNES

THE ECONOMIC CONSEQUENCES
OF THE PEACE

It was not only that the peace-makers seemed to have all but invited a
whole series of future political conflicts. They also, the critics charged, had
failed in dealing with the war's economic aftermath. Where, asked another
member of the British delegation—the famous monetary expert and econo-
mist John Maynard Keynes (1883–1946)—were the provisions for rebuilding
Europe's war-shattered economy?

EUROPE AFTER THE TREATY

This chapter must be one of pessimism. The treaty includes no
provisions for the economic rehabilitation of Europe—nothing to
make the defeated Central empires into good neighbours, nothing
to stabilise the new states of Europe, nothing to reclaim Russia; nor
does it promote in any way a compact of economic solidarity
amongst the Allies themselves; no arrangement was reached at
Paris for restoring the disordered finances of France and Italy, or to
adjust the systems of the Old World and the New.

The Council of Four paid no attention to these issues, being
preoccupied with others—Clemenceau to crush the economic life of
his enemy, Lloyd George to do a deal and bring home something
which would pass muster for a week, the President to do nothing

Source: John Maynard Keynes, *The Economic Consequences of the Peace* (Macmillan and Co.,
London, 1920), pp. 211–212.

that was not just and right. It is an extraordinary fact that the fundamental economic problem of a Europe starving and disintegrating before their eyes, was the one question in which it was impossible to arouse the interest of the Four. Reparation was their main excursion into the economic field, and they settled it as a problem of theology, of politics, of electoral chicane, from every point of view except that of the economic future of the states whose destiny they were handling. . . .

4.

THE TREATY OF LOCARNO

Yet the critics were too harsh, the judgments too pessimistic. For one thing, just what would a just peace have looked like? The peace-makers were dealing with facts, not with abstractions, and in the harsh world of facts, Austria-Hungary's injustice was Czechoslovakia's justice. To have done more for Germany on the matter of Alsace would have meant doing less for France; to have been kinder to the states that had held Polish territory would have been very unkind, and unjust, to Poland. For another thing, while depression and inflation did follow in the wake of the war, Europe did recover by the mid-twenties, and by the end of the decade was considerably more prosperous than it had been in 1914. And beyond that, there was a new spirit of diplomatic reconciliation and political cooperation. One of its most concrete expressions was the Locarno pact of 1925, in which the war's bitterest enemies, Germany, France, and Belgium, voluntarily agreed to respect the borders drawn (or, as the Germans once put it, imposed) in 1918, with Britain and Italy acting as guarantors of the agreement.

(1) FINAL PROTOCOL
OF THE LOCARNO CONFERENCE, 1925.

The representatives of the German, Belgian, British, French, Italian, Polish, and Czechoslovak Governments, who have met at Locarno from the 5th to 16th October, 1925, in order to seek by

Source: C. A. Macartney and others, ed., *Survey of International Affairs*, 1925, Vol. II (Oxford University Press, London, 1928), pp. 439–442.

common agreement means for preserving their respective nations from the scourge of war and for providing for the peaceful settlement of disputes of every nature which might eventually arise between them,

Have given their approval to the draft treaties and conventions which respectively affect them and which, framed in the course of the present conference, are mutually interdependent:-

> Treaty between Germany, Belgium, France, Great Britain, and Italy (Annex A).
> Arbitration Convention between Germany and Belgium (Annex B).
> Arbitration Convention between Germany and France (Annex C).
> Arbitration Treaty between Germany and Poland (Annex D).
> Arbitration Treaty between Germany and Czechoslovakia (Annex E).

These instruments, hereby initialed *ne varietur,* will bear to-day's date, the representatives of the interested parties agreeing to meet in London on the 1st December next, to proceed during the course of a single meeting to the formality of the signature of the instruments which affect them.

The Minister for Foreign Affairs of France states that as a result of the draft arbitration treaties mentioned above, France, Poland, and Czechoslovakia have also concluded at Locarno draft agreements in order reciprocally to assure to themselves the benefit of the said treaties. These agreements will be duly deposited at the League of Nations, but M. Briand holds copies forthwith at the disposal of the Powers represented here.

The Secretary of State for Foreign Affairs of Great Britain proposes that, in reply to certain requests for explanations concerning article 16 of the Covenant of the League of Nations presented by the Chancellor and the Minister for Foreign Affairs of Germany, a letter, of which the draft is similarly attached (Annex F) should be addressed to them at the same time as the formality of signature of the above-mentioned instruments takes place. This proposal is agreed to.

The representatives of the Governments represented here declare their firm conviction that the entry into force of these treaties and conventions will contribute greatly to bring about a moral relaxation of the tension between nations, that it will help powerfully towards the solution of many political or economic problems in accordance with the interests and sentiments of peoples, and that, in strengthening peace and security in Europe, it will hasten on effectively the disarmament provided for in article 8 of the Covenant of the League of Nations.

They undertake to give their sincere co-operation to the work relating to disarmament already undertaken by the League of Nations and to seek the realization thereof in a general agreement.

Done at Locarno, the 16th October, 1925.

> LUTHER.
>
> STRESEMANN.
>
> EMILE VANDERVELDE.
>
> ARI. BRIAND.
>
> AUSTEN CHAMBERLAIN.
>
> BENITO MUSSOLINI.
>
> AL. SKRZYNSKI.
>
> EDUARD BENES.

(2) ANNEX A: TREATY OF MUTUAL GUARANTEE BETWEEN GERMANY, BELGIUM, FRANCE, GREAT BRITAIN, AND ITALY.

The President of the German Reich, His Majesty the King of the Belgians, the President of the French Republic, and His Majesty the King of the United Kingdom of Great Britain and Ireland and of the British Dominions beyond the Seas, Emperor of India, His Majesty the King of Italy;

Anxious to satisfy the desire for security and protection which animates the peoples upon whom fell the scourge of the war of 1914–18;

Taking note of the abrogation of the treaties for the neutralization of Belgium, and conscious of the necessity of ensuring peace in the area which has so frequently been the scene of European conflicts;

Animated also with the sincere desire of giving to all the signatory Powers concerned supplementary guarantees within the framework of the Covenant of the League of Nations and the treaties in force between them;

Have determined to conclude a treaty with these objects, and have appointed as their plenipotentiaries: [names omitted]

Who, having communicated their full powers, found in good and due form, have agreed as follows:-

Article I. The high contracting parties collectively and severally guarantee, in the manner provided in the following articles, the maintenance of the territorial *status quo* resulting from the frontiers between Germany and Belgium and between Germany and France and the inviolability of the said frontiers as fixed by or in pursuance of the Treaty of Peace signed at Versailles on the 28th June, 1919, and also the observance of the stipulations of articles 42 and 43 of the said treaty concerning the demilitarized zone.

Article 2. Germany and Belgium, and also Germany and France, mutually undertake that they will in no case attack or invade each other or resort to war against each other. . . .

Article 3. In view of the undertakings entered into in article 2 of the present treaty, Germany and Belgium and Germany and France undertake to settle by peaceful means and in the manner laid down herein all questions of every kind which may arise between them and which it may not be possible to settle by the normal methods of diplomacy:

Any question with regard to which the parties are in conflict as to their respective rights shall be submitted to judicial decision, and the parties undertake to comply with such decision.

All other questions shall be submitted to a conciliation commission. If the proposals of this commission are not accepted by the two parties, the question shall be brought before the Council of the League of Nations, which will deal with it in accordance with article 15 of the Covenant of the League.

The detailed arrangements for effecting such peaceful settlement are the subject of special agreements signed this day.

Article 4. (1) If one of the high contracting parties alleges that a violation of article 2 of the present treaty or a breach of articles 42 or 43 of the Treaty of Versailles has been or is being committed, it shall bring the question at once before the Council of the League of Nations. . . .

Article 5. The provisions of article 3 of the present treaty are placed under the guarantee of the high contracting parties . . .

Where one of the powers referred to in article 3 without committing a violation of article 2 of the present treaty or a breach of articles 42 or 43 of the Treaty of Versailles, refuses to submit a dispute to peaceful settlement or to comply with an arbitral or judicial decision, the other party shall bring the matter before the Council of the League of Nations, and the Council shall propose what steps shall be taken; the high contracting parties shall comply with these proposals. . . .

In faith whereof the above-mentioned plenipotentiaries have signed the present treaty.

Done at Locarno, the 16th October, 1925.

> LUTHER.
>
> STRESEMANN.
>
> EMILE VANDERVELDE.
>
> A. BRIAND.
>
> AUSTEN CHAMBERLAIN.
>
> BENITO MUSSOLINI.

5.

THE KELLOGG-BRIAND PACT

In return for accepting—this time freely—the new borders in the West, Germany was admitted to the League of Nations. Beyond that, reparations requirements were successively lightened. It was clear that the defeated and despised enemy was on the way to becoming an equal partner again. That was one way of coping with the war and its aftermath. The other was to make a repetition of 1914 impossible. To that end, the world's powers, led by the United States and France, in 1928 signed an agreement that outlawed war as a means of policy.

The President of the German Reich, the President of the United States of America, His Majesty the King of the Belgians, the

Source: Treaties, Conventions, International Acts, Protocols, and Agreements Between the United States and Other Powers, 1923–1937, IV (United States Government Printing Office, Washington, D.C., 1938), pp. 5131–5133.

President of the French Republic, His Majesty the King of Great Britain, Ireland and the British Dominions beyond the Seas, Emperor of India, His Majesty the King of Italy, His Majesty the Emperor of Japan, the President of the Republic of Poland, the President of the Czechoslovak Republic,

Deeply sensible of their solemn duty to promote the welfare of mankind;

Persuaded that the time has come when a frank renunciation of war as an instrument of national policy should be made to the end that the peaceful and friendly relations now existing between their peoples may be perpetuated;

Convinced that all changes in their relations with one another should be sought only by pacific means and be the result of a peaceful and orderly process, and that any signatory Power which shall hereafter seek to promote its national interests by resort to war should be denied the benefits furnished by this Treaty;

Hopeful that, encouraged by their example, all the other nations of the world will join in this humane endeavor and by adhering to the present Treaty as soon as it comes into force bring their peoples within the scope of its beneficent provisions, thus uniting the civilized nations of the world in a common renunciation of war as an instrument of their national policy;

Have decided to conclude a Treaty and for that purpose have appointed as their respective Plenipotentiaries:

[Here follow the names of the plenipotentiaries.]

Who, having communicated to one another their full powers found in good and due form have agreed upon the following articles:

ARTICLE I. The High Contracting Parties solemnly declare in the names of their respective peoples that they condemn recourse to war for the solution of international controversies, and renounce it as an instrument of national policy in their relations with one another.

ARTICLE II. The High Contracting Parties agree that the settlement or solution of all disputes or conflicts of whatever nature or of whatever origin they may be, which may arise among them, shall never be sought except by pacific means.

ARTICLE III. The present Treaty shall be ratified by the High Contracting Parties named in the Preamble in accordance with their respective constitutional requirements, and shall take effect as between them as soon as all their several instruments of ratification shall have been deposited at Washington.

This Treaty shall, when it has come into effect as prescribed in the preceding paragraph, remain open as long as may be necessary for adherence by all the other Powers of the world. Every instrument evidencing the adherence of a Power shall be deposited at Washington and the Treaty shall immediately upon such deposit become effective as between the Power thus adhering and the other Powers parties hereto.

It shall be the duty of the Government of the United States to furnish each Government named in the Preamble and every Government subsequently adhering to this Treaty with a certified copy of the Treaty and of every instrument of ratification or adherence. It shall also be the duty of the Government of the United States telegraphically to notify such Governments immediately upon the deposit with it of each instrument of ratification or adherence.

In faith whereof the respective Plenipotentiaries have signed this Treaty in the French and English languages both texts having equal force, and hereunto affix their seals.

Done at Paris, the twenty-seventh day of August in the year one thousand nine hundred and twenty-eight.

(Signed)

GUSTAV STRESEMANN.

FRANK B. KELLOGG.

PAUL HYMANS.

ARI BRIAND.

CUSHENDUN.

W. L. MACKENZIE KING.

A. J. MCLACHLAN.

C. J. PARR.

J. S. SMIT.

LIAM T. MACCOSGAIR.

CUSHENDUN.

G. MANZONI.

UCHIDA.

AUGUST ZALESKI.

DR. EDUARD BENES.

NOTE BY THE DEPARTMENT OF STATE

ADHERING COUNTRIES

When this Treaty became effective on July 24, 1929, the instruments of ratification of all of the signatory powers having been deposited at Washington, the following countries, having deposited instruments of definitive adherence, became parties to it:

Afghanistan	Finland	Peru
Albania	Guatemala	Portugal
Austria	Hungary	Rumania
Bulgaria	Iceland	Russia
China	Latvia	Kingdom of the Serbs,
Cuba	Liberia	Croats and Slovenes
Denmark	Lithuania	Siam
Dominican Republic	Netherlands	Spain
Egypt	Nicaragua	Sweden
Estonia	Norway	Turkey
Ethiopia	Panama	

6.

ADOLF HITLER

TWO SPEECHES

There was something naïve about the idea of outlawing war by a simple statement of intent, of course. (Where, after all, was the penalty for violating the treaty? Yet what other ultimate penalty could there be but war itself?) On the other hand, the mood of the time was so pacifist, was so appalled by the thought of settling the next diplomatic crisis by another Verdun, that even

Hitchcock, New York, 1941), pp. 312–313 and 332–333; and Erhard Klöss, ed., *Reden des Führers, Politik und Propaganda Adolf Hitlers 1922–1945* (Deutscher Taschenbuch-Verlag, Munich, 1967), p. 191 (translated by the editor).

those who intended to do just that had to pay lip service to the cause of peace. Thus Hitler, in many a public speech, insisted on his abhorrence of war. The first passage is from a Reichstag speech given in 1935, the second from a speech three years later, at the height of the Sudeten crisis, when his aggressive intent had become quite plain.

L I E S

May 21, 1935: . . . The blood shed on the European Continent in the course of the last 300 years bears no proportion to the national result of the events. In the end France has remained France, Germany Germany, Poland Poland, and Italy Italy. What dynastic egoism, political passion, and patriotic blindness have attained in the way of apparently far-reaching political changes by shedding rivers of blood has, as regards national feeling, done no more than touched the skin of the nations. It has not substantially altered their fundamental characters. If these States had applied merely a fraction of their sacrifices to wiser purposes the success would certainly have been greater and more permanent.

When I, as a National Socialist, advocate this view perfectly frankly, I am also influenced by the following realization. The principal effect of every war is to destroy the flower of the nation. But as there is no longer any unoccupied space in Europe, every victory—without making any difference to the fundamental distress in Europe—can at best result in a quantitative increase in the number of the inhabitants of a country. But if the nations attach so much value to that, they can achieve it without tears in a simpler and more natural way. A sound social policy, by increasing the readiness of a nation to have children, can give its own people more children in a few years than the number of aliens that could be conquered and made subject to that nation by war.

No! Nationalist Socialist Germany wants peace because of its fundamental convictions. And it wants peace also owing to the realization of the simple primitive fact that no war would be likely essentially to alter the distress in Europe. It would probably increase it. . . .

Germany needs peace and desires peace. . . .

I cannot better conclude my speech of today to you, my fellow-fighters and trustees of the nation, than by repeating our confession of faith in peace. The nature of our new constitution makes it possible for us in Germany to put a stop to the machinations of war agitators. May the other nations too be able to give bold expression to their real inner longing for peace. *Whoever lights the torch of war in Europe can wish for nothing but chaos.* We, however, live in the firm conviction that in our time will be fulfilled, not the decline but the renaissance of the West. That Germany may make an imperishable contribution to this great work is our proud hope and our unshakable belief.

September 26, 1938. . . . I have been approaching all seemingly insoluble problems with the firm will of settling them peacefully, even at the risk of more or less heavy German concessions. I am a soldier who has fought in the frontlines, and I know how serious a matter war is. I have wanted to spare the German people that experience. I therefore tackled problem after problem with the firm desire of trying everything I could that would make a peaceful solution possible. . . .

LIES

CHAPTER TWO

Challenge and Response: Aggression and Appeasement

1.

ANDRÉ FRANÇOIS-PONCET*

TO JOSEPH PAUL-BONCOUR**

The relationship between truth and fiction in Hitler's speeches was a casual one. In reality, he was all too ready to abandon peace. So now were others. The emergence of strong and aggressive regimes in the thirties meant that the hopes of the twenties had been an illusion. It began with Japan's invasion of Manchuria in 1931, and continued with Italy's war on Ethiopia in 1935, and the intervention of Germany, Italy, and the Soviet Union in Spain's civil war a year later. To many, the most menacing of the new strong men would be Adolf Hitler, though when he first came to power in January 1933, there was considerable question still about just what his true motives were. Who was he? What did he want? Was he as intent on conquest as some of his earlier writings indicated, or as desirous of conciliation as some of his later statements suggested? One of the most acute of foreign observers, the French ambassador André François-Poncet, reflects some of the puzzlement that affected even the best-informed of witnesses, in a report he sent to Paris shortly after Hitler's appointment as chancellor.

To begin with, we should not forget that we are dealing with a self-taught man. The last teachers he knew were those in secondary school. Since he quit high school, he went to hear many a lecture, and all of them left their imprint on his mind. Vast general theories, which open a free field for the imagination, have beguiled him more than scientific facts or historical materialism. The racist theories of Gobineau, the conclusions which Lagarde and Houston Stewart Chamberlain drew from them, Nietzsche's ideas of the will, all have left profound traces on his mind. He gets drunk on words, his own and others'. His convictions, once acquired, remain immutable, and with a passionate logic, which constitutes one of his most salient traits, he pushes his ideas to their most extreme consequences. All objectivity, all understanding of a set of ideas different from his are absolutely alien to him. If intelligence consists essentially of a critical mind, Hitler is not intelligent. But his desire is for action, and his mind possesses the form of intelligence which can be much more useful for a tribune, a leader. He never fails in his unending repetition of the same arguments, even the most

Source: Documents diplomatiques français, 1932–1939, Series I, Vol. I (Imprimerie Nationale, Paris, 1964), pp. 580 and 583–584 (translated by the editor).

* Ambassador of France in Berlin.
** Minister of Foreign Affairs.

threadbare; he drives them as with a hammer into the heads of his audience—and that audience, according to the fine observation of Konrad Heiden, one of the best historians of the racist movement, will imagine in all good faith, having listened to these ideas for the tenth time, that what they are hearing are the fruits of their own thoughts. There is vast strength, for an agitator, in being entirely deaf to the arguments of the other side, and to be able, in Charles Péguy's formula, "always to repeat the same thing, since it always *is* the same thing. . . ."

What direction will he give to his country's foreign policy? On this point, his doctrine fluctuates just as it does in other matters. If today, and indeed for a number of months now, the National Socialist movement, absorbed as it was in Germany's domestic battles, seemed somewhat disinterested in diplomatic problems, it should not be forgotten that from 1927 to 1931 all its propaganda effort was based primarily on the hatred of France, on the ending of reparations, and treaty revision, yet there was a time in 1921 when, out of hatred for Bolshevism as well as out of respect for the continent's principal military power, Hitler made an appeal to France and its feeling of European solidarity to oppose Communism. In that period, England was his villain. Now, the country of Lord Rothermere finds itself the recipient of the Führer's favors almost as much as the Hungary of Admiral Horthy or the Italy of Signor Mussolini. Above all, Hitler's foreign policy is pro-Italian. To align himself with Fascism, Hitler did not hesitate to sacrifice, in 1923, the Germans of South Tyrol, on the pretext that Italian friendship was worth more than a hundred thousand or so Germans annexed by Rome South of the Brenner. Today, it seems, the alliance with Rome remains the keystone to Hitler's diplomanic edifice.

The renaissance of the German fatherland at home and abroad; the destruction of all the "claims" imposed on Germany by the defeat of 1918, by the revolution and by the shortcomings of the governments that followed it; the defense against Communism, "Marxism," and socialist materialism; the purge of the civil service; the reaction against "intellectual Bolshevism"; an honorable restoration of the virtues of family life and of Christianity; a return to corporate bodies as opposed to parliamentary institutions; the battle against the "tyranny of international capital"—all these are essential articles in Hitler's creed. Words whose rhetorical uses are obvious, which makes them no less apt to please the crowds. For they respond to those tendencies, to those hidden needs, which Hitler has known how to uncover. One should not forget that he is not a man of the past, that his aim is not, like that of M. Hugenberg,[1] simply to restore the state of affairs of 1914. In a very significant phrase, Hitler showed his contempt for certain aspects of pre-war German life. "One reason Wagner was so great," he said, "is that on his tombstone one will not read the words, 'Here lies His Excellency, Herr Baron von Wagner, Member of the Privy Council and State Music Director.'"

Hitler is a man of today. . . .

2.   ADOLF HITLER

MEIN KAMPF

What Hitler wanted was indeed considerably more than what his old-fashioned Conservative allies did. His major foreign policy aims were twofold. One was direct, immediate, and entirely nonnegotiable. This was the union of his native Austria with the German Reich. The other was long range, and somewhat more flexible. This was the acquisition of large territories in the East, which would be colonized by German settlers. It was more flexible in the sense that whether he would have the Poles, or the Rumanians, as allies or as enemies were tactical matters, adaptable to the circumstances of the moment. But the core of his grand design in the East really was an immutable as his Austrian program: The ultimate prize was European Russia, with the rich soil of the Crimea and the Ukraine. In *Mein Kampf*, the autobiographical volume he wrote, or dictated, in Landsberg prison in 1924, he was as outspoken about his intentions as he was about the likely need for war in order to achieve them:

. . . German Austria must return to the great German mother country, but not for any economic reasons. No and no again. Even

---

[1] Hitler's Conservative ally, the leader of the German Nationalist party.

Source: Adolf Hitler, *Mein Kampf* (Franz Eher, Munich, 1939), pp. 1 and 736–743 (translated by the editor).

if, from an economic perspective, this union were to make no difference; yes, even if it were harmful, it would have to take place nonetheless. *Common blood belongs in a common Reich.* As long as the German people cannot even manage to unite its own sons in a common state, it has no moral right to colonizing activity. Only when the borders of the Reich include every last German, and the ability to assure his food supply no longer exists, will there arise, from the nation's dire need, the moral right to acquire foreign soil and foreign territory. The plow will then become the sword, and from the tears of war will grow posterity's daily bread. . . .

    . . . To demand the borders of 1914 is political nonsense to such degree and consequence that it appears a crime. . . . The borders of 1914 meant nothing to the German nation. . . . We National Socialists, by contrast, must without wavering keep to our foreign policy aim, which is *to secure to the German nation the soil and space to which it is entitled on this earth.* And this action is the only one which, before God and German generations to come, will justify an investment of blood. Before God, since we have been placed in this world destined to engage in an eternal struggle for our daily bread, as creatures who will not receive anything for nothing and who owe their position as lords of the earth only to their genius and to the courage with which they will fight for and defend it; before German generations to come, since we will have spilled no citizen's blood which will not allow a thousand others to live in future. The soil, on which in times to come generations of German farmers will be able to procreate strong sons, will sanction risking the lives of the sons of today and will, in future ages, absolve the statesmen responsible— even if the present generation should persecute them—of blood guilt and of national sacrifice. . . .

    . . . *Thus we National Socialists consciously put an end to the foreign policy of our prewar period. We begin again where things ended six centuries ago. We put a stop to the eternal drive of the Teuton toward Europe's South and West, and cast our eyes to the land in the East. We finally halt the colonial and economic policies of the prewar period, and move on to the territorial policy of the future.*

    But if we speak of new soil and territory in Europe today, we can think primarily only of Russia and of the subject states bordering it.

    Fate itself seems to wish to give us a hint here. By surrendering Russia to Bolshevism, it robbed the Russian people of that intelligence which, in the past, created and safeguarded Russia's existence as a state. For the organization of a Russian state was not the result of the political abilities of Russia's Slavs. Rather, it was a magnificent example of the political creativity of the Germanic element amid an inferior race. In this fashion, many a powerful empire of this world has been built. Inferior nations with Germanic organizers and masters in command have more than once grown into powerful states and have survived as long as the racial core of the state-creating race remained intact. For centuries, Russia fed on this Teutonic core of its upper, leading strata. Today, this core is almost totally exterminated and destroyed. Its place has been taken by the Jew. But just as it is impossible for the Russian himself, out of his own strength, to rid himself of the Jewish yoke, so it is impossible for the Jew to preserve, in the long run, this mighty empire. He is not a force of organization, but of decomposition. The huge empire in the East is ready to collapse. . . .

Our task, however—the mission of the National Socialist movement—is to make our own people see that its aim for the future will be fulfilled not by the intoxication of a new Alexandrian campaign, but by the steady labor of the German plow, which merely needs to be given land by the sword. . . .

3. NEVILLE CHAMBERLAIN

AT THE LORD MAYOR'S BANQUET

But perhaps these were phantasies. *Mein Kampf* was full of odd daydreams expressed in murky prose. Hitler was chancellor now, a man of responsibility, who repeatedly said that what he wanted was peace and conciliation. It was true that in 1935 he rearmed Germany in violation of the Versailles treaty, that he remilitarized the Rhineland and sent a small German air force to Spain that bombed troops and towns in that country's civil war. And it was true that his Axis partner, Italy, was committing open aggression

Source: Neville Chamberlain, *In Search of Peace* (G. P. Putnam's Sons, New York, 1939), p. 29.

in Ethiopia. Yet it seemed to the statesmen of the West that the wisest course to follow was one of dealing with both Hitler and Mussolini by peaceable means, by negotiating each issue—appeasement was the word being used. Many motives accounted for that policy. There was the prevailing pacifism of the period. Even if Hitler should invade Great Britain, said Bertrand Russell (without the least intent of irony), the Nazis should be welcomed like tourists, for "whatever damage the Germans could do to us would not be worse than the damage done in fighting them, even if we won." Nor would the damage be very great. "The Nazis would find some interest in our way of living, I think, and the starch would be taken out of them." [1] Then there was the fear of bolshevism, and the terrible suspicion—or conviction—that if another European war were to break out, only Russia would gain from it. Don't let matters get out of hand, warned a British foreign secretary (and the French tended to follow the British lead), "for then the only ones to profit would be the communists." There was the idea that Britain and France, if they maintained a neutral stance, could mediate in future crises and keep them from turning into another Sarajevo. But above all, there was the memory of 1914–1918, the urge to maintain the peace. Neville Chamberlain, Britain's prime minister and chief architect of its foreign policy from 1937 to 1940, expressed that thought when he addressed the lord mayor's banquet in London's Guildhall on November 9, 1937:

. . . Perhaps I may put my subject in the form of a question. What sort of future are we trying to create for ourselves and for our children? Is it to be better or worse than that which we have inherited? Are we trying to make a world in which the peoples that inhabit it shall be able to live out their lives in peace of mind and in the enjoyment of a constantly rising standard of all that makes life worth living, of health and comfort, of recreation, and of culture? Or are we preparing for ourselves a future which is to be one perpetual nightmare, filled with the constant dread of the horrors of war, forced to bury ourselves below ground and to spend all our substance upon the weapons of destruction?

One has only to state these two alternatives to be sure that human nature, which is the same all the world over, must reject the nightmare with all its might and cling to the only prospect which can give happiness. And for any Government deliberately to deny to their people what must be their plainest and simplest right would be to betray their trust and to call down upon their heads the condemnation of all mankind.

[1] The New York Times, April 2, 1937, p. 9.

I do not believe that such a Government anywhere exists among civilised peoples. I am convinced that the aim of every statesman worthy the name, to whatever country he belongs, must be the happiness of the people for whom and to whom he is responsible, and in that faith I am sure that a way can, and will, be found to free the world from the curse of armaments and the fears that give rise to them and to open up a happier and a wiser future for mankind.

4.   NEVILLE CHAMBERLAIN

"TO MAKE GENTLE
THE LIFE OF THE WORLD"

Of course that was before Hitler moved against Austria in the spring of 1938, thus making the first of the *Mein Kampf* phantasies come true. But neither Britain nor France quite saw it that way. Rather, the Western reaction was to deplore the manner of the Austrian takeover, but to accept its essence. If Hitler wished to extend his rule to those who so frantically welcomed it, and who considered themselves as German as Hessians or Bavarians, what moral right did other powers have to oppose him? Instead, as Chamberlain put it, it now was as imperative as ever that "if you want to secure a peace which can be relied on to last, you have got to find out what are the causes of war and remove them." The enforced separation of German Austria from the Reich had been one such potential cause, and it was gone now—removed in Hitler's brutal fashion, but removed. In a speech he gave at Birmingham not quite four weeks after German troops had moved into Vienna on April 8, 1938, Chamberlain once more outlined the reasons and the principles behind appeasement.

. . . You may have read that at the beginning of this week we had in the House of Commons a debate, a rather lively debate, on foreign affairs. That was only the last of a whole series of debates on that subject, and, although we are told nowadays that people do not

Source: Chamberlain, *In Search of Peace,* pp. 96–98 and 102.

read of what goes on in the House of Commons, I cannot help thinking that the general outlines of the Government's foreign policy are fairly freely read.

We are bound by certain treaties, entered into with general approval, to go to the assistance of France and of Belgium in the event of unprovoked aggression against either of those two countries. But we have declined to commit ourselves to a similar undertaking in respect of other countries farther away, in which our vital interests are not concerned to the same extent, and which might be involved in war under conditions over which we would have no control. Now it is quite true that in these days no one can say where or when a war will end once it has begun, or what Governments may ultimately be entangled in a dispute which originally might have been confined to some remote corner of Europe. But at least we ought to reserve to ourselves the right to say whether we consider it necessary to enter into such a war or not, and we ought not to hand over to others the determination of our action when it might involve such tremendous consequences to ourselves.

Sometimes we are told that if only we took a bolder course, if we were to lay down here and now precisely the circumstances in which we would or would not go to war, we should give such a warning to the world that there would in fact be no war. That would be a gamble, and it would be a gamble not with money, but with the lives of men, women and children of our own race and blood. I am not prepared to enter into a gamble of that kind, and though the stern necessity for war may arise in the future, as it has risen in the past, I would not give the word for it unless I were absolutely convinced that in no other way could we preserve our liberty.

Then there are other critics who say they cannot understand what the policy of His Majesty's Government is, and they conclude therefore that there can be no policy. You may remember what Johnson said to a man who said he could not understand his reasoning: "Sir, I can give you a reason, but I cannot give you understanding." Our policy has been stated often enough and clearly enough, but nevertheless, I will state it again to-night. But before I come to that, I would like to say to you what our policy is not.

Our policy is not one of dividing Europe into two opposing *blocs* of countries, each arming against the other amidst a growing flood of illwill on both sides, which can only end in war. That seems to us to be a policy which is dangerous and stupid. You may say we may not approve of dictatorships. I think, perhaps, most of us in this room do not approve of them, but there they are. You cannot remove them. We have to live with them, and to us in the Government it seems that, while we must continue to arm until we can get a general agreement to disarm, it is only common sense that in the meantime we should try to establish friendly relations with any country that is willing to be friends with us. We should take any and every opportunity to try to remove any genuine and legitimate grievances that may exist.

During the recent weeks we have been engaging in conversations for this purpose with the Italian Government, with the result that a whole cloud of suspicions and misunderstandings has been blown away. There is to-day a good prospect of restoring those old friendly relations which, until they were recently broken, had lasted so long that they had become almost traditional between our two countries.

Anyone would think that such a happy change as that, such a lightening of the tension, such a prospect of getting rid of a state of feeling which was becoming a menace both to Italy and ourselves, would have been welcomed everywhere, and yet the whole of the Opposition, the Socialists and Liberals, with the notable exception of the veteran George Lansbury and George's friends who have the courage to express their approval, have denounced these conversations with the utmost bitterness. They have painted the most fantastic pictures of the subjects which we are supposed to be discussing. They have talked about vast loans, about surrenders to dictators, about the gullibility of the Prime Minister in believing a single word that was said to him, and even declare that they believe we were going to sacrifice the British Empire itself in a panic.

I only ask you to have a little patience, to wait a little longer—and I do not think it will be very much longer—before our agreement with Italy is concluded and published, and then, if you are not of my opinion, if you do not believe that it is not the Prime Minister who has been fooled, but the Socialists and Liberals who have fooled themselves, I will be prepared to eat my hat.

No, believe me, the Government have a very clear and definite foreign policy, which they keep always before them, and which they continue to pursue by various methods according to the circumstances of the time. The object of that policy is to maintain peace and to give confidence to the people, if that be possible, that peace will be maintained so that they may all go about their occupations free from a sense of menace lurking always in the background.

. . . [There] is no need to look forward to the future with apprehension, and still less with despair. We pass no judgment here on the political systems of other countries, but neither Fascism nor Communism is in harmony with our temperament and creed. We will have nothing to do with either of them here. And yet, whatever differences there may be between us and other nations on that subject, do not forget that we are all members of the human race and subject to the like passions and affections and fears and desires. There must be something in common between us if only we can find it, and perhaps by our aloofness from the rest of Europe we may have some special part to play as conciliator and mediator. An ancient historian once wrote of the Greeks that they had made gentle the life of the world. I do not know whether in these modern days it is possible for any nation to emulate the example of the Greeks, but I can imagine no nobler ambition for an English statesman than to win the same tribute for his own country.

5.   WINSTON CHURCHILL

"A PROGRAM OF AGGRESSION"

Not everyone agreed with the prime minister. Among his most vocal opponents was Winston Churchill. Hitler, warned Churchill, was engaged in a systematic program of aggression, and no one should be deluded into thinking that he merely wished to correct the inequities of Versailles or to protect fellow-Germans abroad. In the spring of 1938—on March 14, the day after Austria had been incorporated into the German Reich—Churchill rose in the House of Commons to say that the time to resist Hitler had plainly

Source: Parliamentary Debates, House of Commons, Fifth Series, vol. 333 (His Majesty's Stationary Office, London, 1938), pp. 95–100.

come. For if England should fail to abandon appeasement, "continued resistance and true collective security would become impossible." He then went on to say:

The gravity of the event of 11th March[1] cannot be exaggerated. Europe is confronted with a programme of aggression, nicely calculated and timed, unfolding stage by stage, and there is only one choice open, not only to us, but to other countries who are unfortunately concerned—either to submit, like Austria, or else to take effective measures while time remains to ward off the danger and, if it cannot be warded off, to cope with it. Resistance will be hard, yet I am persuaded—and the Prime Minister's speech confirms me—that it is to this conclusion of resistance to overweening encroachment that His Majesty's Government will come, and the House of Commons will certainly sustain them in playing a great part in the effort to preserve the peace of Europe, and, if it cannot be preserved, to preserve the freedom of the nations of Europe. If we were to delay, if we were to go on waiting upon events for a considerable period, how much should we throw away of resources which are now available for our security and for the maintenance of peace? How many friends would be alienated, how many potential allies should we see go, one by one, down the grisly gulf, how many times would bluff succeed, until behind bluff ever-gathering forces had accumulated reality? Where are we going to be two years hence, for instance, when the German Army will certainly be much larger than the French Army, and when all the small nations will have fled from Geneva to pay homage to the ever-waxing power of the Nazi system, and to make the best terms they can for themselves?

. . . Why not make a stand while there is still a good company of united, very powerful countries that share our dangers and aspirations? Why should we delay until we are confronted with a general landslide of those small countries passing over, because they have no other choice, to the overwhelming power of the Nazi régime?

If a number of States were assembled around Great Britain and France in a solemn treaty for mutual defence against aggression; if they had their forces marshaled in what you may call a Grand

---

[1] The day the German troops crossed into Austria.

Alliance; if they had their Staff arrangements concerted; if all this rested, as it can honorably rest, upon the Covenant of the League of Nations, in pursuance of all the purposes and ideals of the League of Nations; if that were sustained, as it would be, by the moral sense of the world; and if it were done in the year 1938—and, believe me, it may be the last chance there will be for doing it—then I say that you might even now arrest this approaching war. Then perhaps the curse which overhangs Europe would pass away. Then perhaps the ferocious passions which now grip a great people would turn inwards and not outwards in an internal rather than an external explosion, and mankind would be spared the deadly ordeal towards which we have been sagging and sliding month by month. I have ventured to indicate a positive conception, a practical and realistic conception, and one which I am convinced will unite all the forces of this country without whose help your armies cannot be filled or your munitions made. Before we cast away this hope, this cause and this plan, which I do not at all disguise has an element of risk, let those who wish to reject it ponder well and earnestly upon what will happen to us if, when all else has been thrown to the wolves, we are left to face our fate alone.

6.   NEVILLE CHAMBERLAIN

"PEACE TO THE LAST MOMENT"

But Churchill spoke for a minority, and appeasement was the policy followed in the next great European crisis. It occurred soon after Austria and centered on Czechoslovakia. Hitler's public position was the same that it had been during the Austrian *Anschluss*. All that he had in mind, said Hitler, was the protection of ethnic Germans—in this case those of Czechoslovakia's Sudeten area. The British, and the French would follow their lead, thought that the issue was negotiable. The preservation of Czechoslovakia's borders was not worth another battle of the Somme. On September 27, at the height of the Sudeten crisis, Chamberlain explained his case to the British public in a national broadcast:

Source: Chamberlain, *In Search of Peace*, pp. 173–175.

To-morrow Parliament is going to meet, and I shall be making a full statement of the events which have led up to the present anxious and critical situation.

An earlier statement would not have been possible when I was flying backwards and forwards across Europe, and the position was changing from hour to hour. But to-day there is a lull for a brief time, and I want to say a few words to you, men and women of Britain and the Empire, and perhaps to others as well.

First of all I must say something to those who have written to my wife or myself in these last weeks to tell us of their gratitude for my efforts and to assure us of their prayers for my success. Most of these letters have come from women—mothers or sisters of our own countrymen. But there are countless others besides—from France, from Belgium, from Italy, even from Germany, and it has been heart-breaking to read of the growing anxiety they reveal and their intense relief when they thought, too soon, that the danger of war was past.

If I felt my responsibility heavy before, to read such letters has made it seem almost overwhelming. How horrible, fantastic, incredible it is that we should be digging trenches and trying on gas masks here because of a quarrel in a far-away country between people of whom we know nothing. It seems still more impossible that a quarrel which has already been settled in principle should be the subject of war.

I can well understand the reasons why the Czech Government have felt unable to accept the terms which have been put before them in the German memorandum. Yet I believe after my talks with Herr Hitler that, if only time were allowed, it ought to be possible for the arrangements for transferring the territory that the Czech Government has agreed to give to Germany to be settled by agreement under conditions which would assure fair treatment to the population concerned.

You know already that I have done all that one man can do to compose this quarrel. After my visits to Germany I have realised vividly how Herr Hitler feels that he must champion other Germans, and his indignation that grievances have not been met before this. He told me privately, and last night he repeated publicly, that after this Sudeten German question is settled, that is the end of Germany's territorial claims in Europe.

After my first visit to Berchtesgaden I did get the assent of the

Czech Government to proposals which gave the substance of what Herr Hitler wanted and I was taken completely by surprise when I got back to Germany and found that he insisted that the territory should be handed over to him immediately, and immediately occupied by German troops without previous arrangements for safeguarding the people within the territory who were not Germans, or did not want to join the German Reich.

I must say that I find this attitude unreasonable. If it arises out of any doubts that Herr Hitler feels about the intentions of the Czech Government to carry out their promises and hand over the territory, I have offered on the part of the British Government to guarantee their words, and I am sure the value of our promise will not be underrated anywhere.

I shall not give up the hope of a peaceful solution, or abandon my efforts for peace, as long as any chance for peace remains. I would not hesitate to pay even a third visit to Germany if I thought it would do any good. But at this moment I see nothing further that I can usefully do in the way of mediation.

Meanwhile there are certain things we can and shall do at home. Volunteers are still wanted for air-raid precautions, for fire brigade and police services, and for the Territorial units. I know that all of you, men and women alike, are ready to play your part in the defence of the country, and I ask you all to offer your services, if you have not already done so, to the local authorities, who will tell you if you are wanted and in what capacity.

Do not be alarmed if you hear of men being called up to man the anti-aircraft defences or ships. These are only precautionary measures, such as a Government must take in times like this. But they do not necessarily mean that we have determined on war or that war is imminent.

However much we may sympathise with a small nation confronted by a big and powerful neighbour, we cannot in all circumstances undertake to involve the whole British Empire in war simply on her account. If we have to fight it must be on larger issues than that. I am myself a man of peace to the depths of my soul. Armed conflict between nations is a nightmare to me; but if I were convinced that any nation had made up its mind to dominate the world by fear of its force, I should feel that it must be resisted. Under such a domination life for people who believe in liberty would not be worth living; but war is a fearful thing, and we must

be very clear, before we embark on it, that it is really the great
issues that are at stake, and that the call to risk everything in their
defence, when all the consequences are weighed, is irresistible.

For the present I ask you to await as calmly as you can the events
of the next few days. As long as war has not begun, there is always
hope that it may be prevented, and you know that I am going to
work for peace to the last moment. Good night.

7.

ADOLF HITLER

"WE WANT NO CZECHS"

Hitler's assurance to which Chamberlain agreed was contained in a
speech he gave to the party faithful in Berlin's Sports Palace on September
26, 1938. In it, he was as unequivocal—and, on the face of it, reasonable—as
in any of his public declarations:

. . . There is not much I have to say. I am grateful to Mr.
Chamberlain for all his efforts. I assured him that the German
people wants nothing but peace. However, I also told him that I
cannot retreat from the limits of our patience.

I further told him, and I repeat this here, that once this problem
is solved, there will be no territorial problem left for Germany in
Europe!

And I further assured him that just as soon as Czecho-Slovakia
will have solved its problems—that is to say as soon as the Czechs
have reached a settlement with their other minorities that is based
on peaceful means and not on oppression—I shall no longer have
any interest in the Czech state. And I will guarantee him that! We
want no Czechs! [Applause]

Source: Völkischer Beobachter, September 27, 1938, p. 3 (translated by the editor).

8.

THE MUNICH AGREEMENT

Did Hitler make the most reliable of witnesses to his own intentions? It did not matter. The West *wished* to believe him. It was better to let the Sudeten Germans join the Reich than to play out 1914 again. On September 29, 1938, the leaders of Germany, Italy, France, and Great Britain put their signatures to the agreement that surrendered the area in question to Germany.

Germany, the United Kingdom, France and Italy, taking into consideration the agreement which has been already reached in principle for the cession to Germany of the Sudeten German territory, have agreed on the following terms and conditions governing the said cession and the measures consequent thereon, and by this agreement they each hold themselves responsible for the steps necessary to secure its fulfilment:

1 The evacuation will begin on October 1st.

2 The United Kingdom, France and Italy agree that the evacuation of the territory shall be completed by October 10th, without any existing installations having been destroyed, and that the Czechoslovak Government will be held responsible for carrying out the evacuation without damage to the said installations.

3 The conditions governing the evacuation will be laid down in detail by an international commission composed of representatives of Germany, the United Kingdom, France, Italy and Czechoslovakia.

4 The occupation by stages of the predominantly German territory by German troops will begin on October 1st. The four territories marked on the attached map will be occupied by German troops in the following order: The territory marked No. I on the 1st and 2nd October, the territory marked No. II on the 2nd and 3rd of October, the territory marked No. III on the 3rd, 4th and 5th of October. The remaining territory of preponderantly German character will be ascertained by the aforesaid international commission forthwith and be occupied by German troops by the 10th of October.

Source: Documents on German Foreign Policy, 1918–1945, Series D, vol. 2 (U.S. Government Printing Office, Washington, D.C., 1949), pp. 1014–1016 and Appendix VII.

5. The international commission referred to in paragraph 3 will determine the territories in which a plebiscite is to be held. These territories will be occupied by international bodies until the plebiscite has been completed. The same commission will fix the conditions in which the plebiscite is to be held, taking as a basis the conditions of the Saar plebiscite. The commission will also fix a date, not later than the end of November, on which the plebiscite will be held.

6 The final determination of the frontiers will be carried out by the international commission. This commission will also be entitled to recommend to the four Powers, Germany, the United Kingdom, France and Italy, in certain exceptional cases minor modifications in the strictly ethnographical determination of the zones which are to be transferred without plebiscite.

7 There will be a right of option into and out of the transferred territories, the option to be exercised within six months from the date of this agreement. A German-Czechoslovak commission shall determine the details of the option, consider ways of facilitating the transfer of population and settle questions of principle arising out of the said transfer.

8 The Czechoslovak Government will, within a period of four weeks from the date of this agreement, release from their military and police forces any Sudeten Germans who may wish to be released, and the Czechoslovak Government will, within the same period, release Sudeten German prisoners who are serving terms of imprisonment for political offences.

ADOLF HITLER
NEVILLE CHAMBERLAIN
Munich,   ED. DALADIER
September 29, 1938   BENITO MUSSOLINI

ANNEX TO THE AGREEMENT

His Majesty's Government in the United Kingdom and the French Government have entered into the above agreement on the basis that they stand by the offer, contained in paragraph 6 of the

Anglo-French proposals of September 19th, relating to an international guarantee of the new boundaries of the Czechoslovak State against unprovoked aggression.

When the question of the Polish and Hungarian minorities in Czechoslovakia has been settled, Germany and Italy for their part will give a guarantee to Czechoslovakia.

	ADOLF HITLER
	NEVILLE CHAMBERLAIN
Munich,	ED. DALADIER
September 29, 1938.	BENITO MUSSOLINI

ADDITIONAL DECLARATION

The Heads of the Governments of the four Powers declare that the problems of the Polish and Hungarian minorities in Czechoslovakia, if not settled within three months by agreement between the respective Governments, shall form the subject of another meeting of the Heads of the Government of the four Powers here present.

	ADOLF HITLER
	NEVILLE CHAMBERLAIN
Munich,	ED. DALADIER
September 29, 1938.	BENITO MUSSOLINI

9.

RUSSIAN PRESS STATEMENTS

The Czechs tried to protest. "Some purely Czech communes and regions," they warned, "will fall to Germany. Minorities are being created in central Europe. The railway and the most important roads are destroyed. Centers of

Source: *Prager Presse*, May 11, 1938, as quoted in *Documents on German Foreign Policy*, Series D, vol. 2, pp. 267–269; and *Pravda*, October 4 and 14, 1938.
* Translated by Nikolai Altenkov and Horst Lorscheider.

great economic and strategic importance, such as Pilsen, Ostrau, Brno, etc., are condemned to stagnation. A million Czechs will be allotted to Germany. The republic becomes impossibly crippled." They were arguing to no avail. There was nothing they could do; nothing was left to them but quiet fury. Munich, as seen from the Czechs' point of view, was as much of a *Diktat* as Versailles had been from the Germans'. The one difference was that the Czechs were not even asked to sign the Munich agreement.

Another power not represented was the Soviet Union, and there has been much speculation, then and since, what the Russians would have done had their aid been requested in support of the Czech Republic. Three short documents, one from the summer of 1938, the other dating from the period immediately following the crisis, make clear the official Soviet attitude—that Russia at no time was afraid to fight, and at all times stood ready to honor its treaty obligations to France and Czechoslovakia.

TO THE LAST LETTER

KALININ ON THE FULFILLMENT OF THE TREATY OBLIGATIONS OF THE SOVIET UNION

On Sunday afternoon [May 8, 1938] Kalinin, Chairman of the Supreme Council of the Soviet Union, received the foreign workers' delegations which had come to Moscow for the 1st of May celebrations. After the welcoming speeches, Kalinin answered various questions, among them a question by Skavnič, the Czech trade union official, who asked whether Kalinin as head of the Soviet Union could reply to the question whether the Soviet Union would come to the aid of Czechoslovakia if the Republic were attacked without provocation and France rendered assistance. Kalinin replied as follows:

"The Soviet Union has always and without reserve honored the treaties concluded with other nations; it would do the same in this case, too, and if necessary would fulfill all its obligations toward Czechoslovakia and France to the last letter. Some French newspapers have written in a vein as if the Franco-Soviet Treaty were of advantage only to the Soviet Union. I do not want to say that this Treaty is not advantageous for the Soviet Union, but it is, and will be, more useful to France. The Soviet Union is a rich country. I do not mean by this that France is not a rich country, for France is even the creditor of a number of other nations. But the Soviet Union has minerals, iron, petroleum, foodstuffs, cotton, and in fact everything necessary for the conduct of any war. And France does not possess all this in the same measure. If the Treaty of Friendship

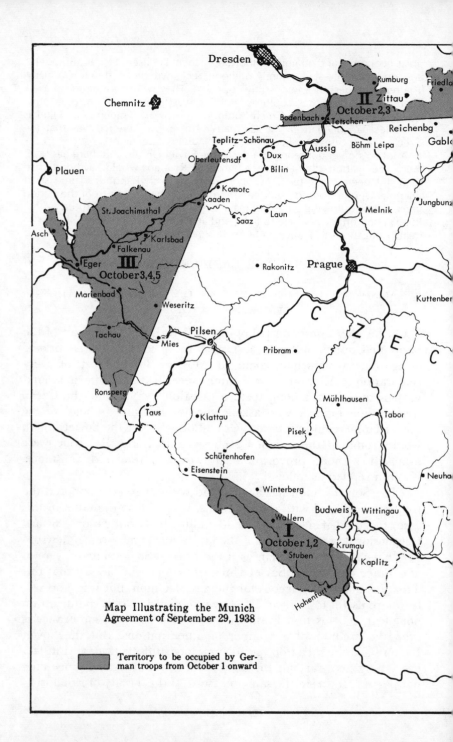

Dresden

Chemnitz

II Zittau
Rumburg
Friedla
October 2,3
Bodenbach Tetschen
Reichenbg
Gabl

Teplitz–Schönau
Böhm Leipa
Oberleutensdf
Dux
Aussig

Plauen
Bilin

Komotc

Kaaden
Jungbunz

St. Joachimsthal
Saaz
Laun
Melnik

Asch
Karlsbad

Falkenau
Rakonitz
Prague

Eger
III

October 3,4,5
Kuttenber

Marienbad
Weseritz

C

Tachau
Pilsen
Z

Mies
Pribram
E

Ronsperg
Mühlhausen
C
Tabor

Taus
Klattau

Pisek

Schütenhofen
Neuha

Eisenstein
Winterberg

Budweis
Wittingau
Wallern

I
Krumau

October 1,2
Kaplitz
Stuben

Hohenfurt

Map Illustrating the Munich
Agreement of September 29, 1938

Territory to be occupied by German troops from October 1 onward

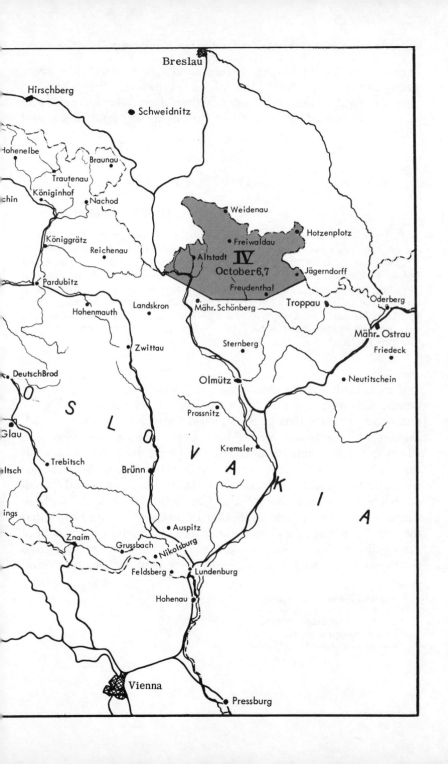

between the Soviet Union, France, and Czechoslovakia were as strong as we wish it to be, then it would influence Britain also to choose other directions for her policy than those so far followed, and the Treaty would have greater international significance and weight."

TASS[1] REPORT

[*Pravda*, October 4, 1938]

The semi-official organ of the Czechoslovak foreign ministry, *Prager Presse*, carried a report from its Paris correspondent in its issue of September 30 under the headline "Paris-London-Moscow," alleging that the French and British governments had kept the Soviet government informed on a regular basis concerning the Czechoslovak question, and that lengthy conversations on this question had been held between M. Bonnet[2] and Comrade Surits,[3] and Lord Halifax[4] and Comrade Maisky.[5] The *Prager Presse* correspondent concludes from this that the Munich agreement "does not represent just a four power pact."

Tass is authorized to state that this report of the *Prager Presse* correspondent is completely at variance with the facts. *Tass* is authorized to state that at the meetings held recently between M. Bonnet and Comrade Surits, and Lord Halifax and Comrade Maisky, the two ambassadors were given no information beyond that published in the daily press. No consultations took place, nor were any agreements made, between the Soviet, French, and British governments on the fate of the Czechoslovak republic and on concessions to the aggressor. Neither France nor England consulted the USSR; instead, they merely informed the Soviet government of accomplished facts. As was already made clear in the *Tass* statement of October 2, the Soviet government did not have, and

[1] The official Soviet news agency.
[2] The French foreign minister.
[3] The Soviet ambassador to Paris.
[4] Britain's foreign secretary.
[5] The Soviet ambassador to London.

does not have, anything to do with the Munich conference and its decisions.

STATEMENT BY THE SOVIET EMBASSY
IN LONDON

[*Pravda*, October 14, 1938]

LONDON, October 13 *(Tass)* The embassy of the USSR in London issued the following statement on October 11, in connection with the speech of the parliamentary secretary of the ministry of aviation, Lord Winterton . . . :

"It is reported in the British press that Lord Winterton stated that at the time of the Czechoslovak crisis, the Soviet Union made no offer to help but, because of its military weakness, confined itself to vague promises.

"This statement by Winterton is a complete distortion of the Soviet government's attitude on the Czechoslovak problem. The position of the USSR in this matter has been clear and concise, leaving no room for doubt. It was outlined by People's Commissar for Foreign Affairs, M. M. Litvinov, in his speech to the League of Nations Assembly on September 21.

"In this speech, summarizing his conversation with the French chargé d'affaires in Moscow on September 2, 1938, Litvinov stated that the USSR intended to carry out all the obligations arising from the Soviet pact with Czechoslovakia, and together with France to give that country all necessary help by all available means. He added that the Soviet military authorities were ready to begin negotiations with representatives of the French and Czechoslovak general staffs immediately, with the aim of devising concrete measures for joint action."

10.

ANGLO-GERMAN DECLARATION OF SEPTEMBER 30, 1938

No such concrete measures were to be discussed. Precisely whose fault this was will remain a matter of controversy, just as much as the Soviets' actual willingness to come to the aid of the Czechs. Not that either question seemed to matter very much at the time. What did, instead, was that Europe remained at peace, and beyond that, that Munich might turn out to be a blessing in disguise by leading to a new era of Anglo-German consultation. In his last meeting with Hitler at Munich, Chamberlain asked for, and unhesitatingly received, a formal expression of the Führer's desire to prevent any future Anglo-German conflict. Here is the conversation leading up to that declaration, and the declaration itself:

Note of a Conversation between the Prime Minister and Herr Hitler, September 30, 1938, at the latter's Flat in Munich.

Prime Minister: He was very pleased at the result of yesterday's proceedings, and he hoped that Herr Hitler was equally happy.

Herr Hitler: He was particularly happy, especially that the hopes of many millions of Germans had now been fulfilled and that the $3\frac{1}{2}$ millions of Sudeten Germans were now going to be once more secure. Their sufferings had indeed been terrible, but now they would be the happiest of all about the result of the conference. In this connection he would like to thank the British Prime Minister once more for his great efforts to bring about a peaceful solution. The most difficult problem of all had now been concluded and his own main task had been happily fulfilled.

Prime Minister: He warmly appreciated Herr Hitler's words, but there was now something he wished to say to him by way of an appeal. He had been told that Herr Hitler intended, if the Czechs accepted the proposals, to treat them very generously. This was what he (the Prime Minister) would have expected from Herr Hitler, but he was obliged to consider the possibility that the Czech Government might be mad enough to refuse the terms and attempt resistance. In such an eventuality he wanted to ask Herr Hitler to

Source: E. L. Woodward and Rohan Butler, ed., *Documents on British Foreign Policy 1919-1939*, Third Series, Vol. II (His Majesty's Stationery Office, London, 1949), pp. 635-640.

make sure that nothing should be done which would diminish the high opinion of him which would be held throughout the world in consequence of yesterday's proceedings. In particular, he trusted that there would be no bombardment of Prague or killing of women and children by attacks from the air.

Herr Hitler: Before answering that specific question, he would like to say something on a point of principle. Years ago he made proposals for the restriction of the use of the air arm. He himself fought in the Great War and has a personal knowledge of what air bombardment means. It had been his intention, if he had to use force, to limit air action to front line zones as a matter of principle, but even if the Czechs were mad enough to reject the terms and he had consequently to take forcible action, he would always try to spare the civilian population and to confine himself to military objectives. He hated the thought of little babies being killed by gas bombs. . . .

[The two men then went on to discuss a variety of issues, including disarmament, after which Chamberlain said:]

Now, he would not keep Herr Hitler any longer, but he wished to say that he thought it would be a pity if this meeting passed off with nothing more than the settlement of the Czech question, which had been agreed upon yesterday. What he had in mind was to suggest to Herr Hitler that it would be helpful to both countries and to the world in general if they could issue some statement which showed the agreement between them on the desirability of better Anglo-German relations, leading to a greater European stability. Accordingly, he had ventured to draft a short statement which he would now ask Herr Hitler to read and to consider whether he would be disposed to issue such a statement over the signatures of himself and the Prime Minister to the public. As these observations were translated to Herr Hitler he ejaculated at intervals 'Ja! Ja!' and when it was finished he said he would certainly agree to sign this document. When did the Prime Minister wish to do so?

The Prime Minister: Immediately.

Herr Hitler: Then let us sign.

At this point, they both rose, went to a writing table and, without

any further words, appended their signatures to the document
(copy attached as Appendix), of which the Prime Minister handed
Herr Hitler one copy to keep and retained the other.

APPENDIX

We, the German Führer and Chancellor and the British Prime
Minister, have had a further meeting to-day and are agreed in
recognising that the question of Anglo-German relations is of the
first importance for the two countries and for Europe.

We regard the agreement signed last night and the Anglo-
German Naval Agreement as symbolic of the desire of our two
peoples never to go to war with one another again.

We are resolved that the method of consultation shall be the
method adopted to deal with any other questions that may concern
our two countries, and we are determined to continue our efforts to
remove possible sources of difference and thus to contribute to
assure the peace of Europe.

(signed) A. HITLER.

September 30, 1938.   (signed) NEVILLE CHAMBERLAIN.

11.   THE TIMES

AN EDITORIAL

Returning to Britain with that document in hand, Chamberlain received a
hero's welcome. Massive criticism of Munich would come later. At the time,
sheer relief over the avoidance of war, and admiration for the prime
minister's peace-keeping efforts, dominated public opinion. "Come straight
to Buckingham Palace," asked the king, "so that I can express to you
personally my most heartfelt congratulations on the success of your visit to
Munich." The streets all along the way from the airport to the palace,
Chamberlain noted, were lined with "people of every class, shouting
themselves hoarse, leaping on the running board, banging on the windows,

Source: The Times, London, Saturday October 1, 1938.

and thrusting their hands into the car to be shaken." Later, under his windows in Downing Street, crowds sang "For he's a jolly good fellow." The press was nearly unanimous in its praise, and from all over the world, the letters poured into Downing Street. Within three weeks of Munich, he had received some 40,000 messages. Some were accompanied by gifts. There were fishing rods by the score, there came 4,000 tulips from Holland, cases of Alsatian wine from France, and from Greece, a request for a piece of his umbrella to make a relic in an icon. An editorial from the London *Times*, which appeared right after the Munich settlement reflects the mood:

A NEW DAWN

No conqueror returning from a victory on the battlefield has come home adorned with nobler laurels than MR. CHAMBER-LAIN from Munich yesterday; and KING and people alike have shown by the manner of their reception their sense of his achievement. The terms of settlement in the Czech-German dispute, reached in the small hours of the morning and published in the later issues of *The Times* of yesterday, had been seen to deliver the world from a menace of extreme horror while doing rough-and-ready justice between the conflicting claims. Yet even this great service to humanity was already beginning to appear as the lesser half of the Prime Minister's work in Munich. He himself announced it as the prelude to a larger settlement. He had not only relegated an agonizing episode to the past; he had found for the nations a new hope for the future. The joint declaration made by Herr Hitler and Mr. Chamberlain proclaims that "the desire of the two peoples never to go to war with one another again" shall henceforth govern the whole of their relationships. There have been times when such a manifesto could be dismissed as a pious platitude, likely to be forgotten long before an occasion could arise for it to be practically tested. The present, it is fair to think, is not such a time. The two statesmen plainly recognize in their declaration that there are still sources of difference between Great Britain and Germany, which for the sake of the peace of Europe must be settled at an early date; it is in direct relation to these that they pledge themselves to the methods of peaceful consultation, and so demonstrate that they expect to be taken at the full value of their word. By inserting a specific reference to the Anglo-German Naval Agreement, as well as to the negotiations so happily concluded at

Munich, the Führer reminds us of an earnest of his good intentions, which the British people, in the new atmosphere, will readily acknowledge.

Civilization had been so near to the brink of collapse that any peaceful issue from the dispute of the last months would have been an overwhelming relief; but close examination of the Munich terms, in particular of the geographical adjustments, shows that they constitute not only a settlement but a hopeful settlement. That they should be bitterly resented in Czechoslovakia must add to the profound sympathy which has always been felt in England with one of the smaller and, as it seemed to many, the more promising countries emerging from the Peace Treaties. Yet the loss of the Sudeten territories had long been unavoidable, nor was it desirable that it should be avoided. That was the opinion not only of all who believed in the theory of self-determination, but of Lord Runciman, who had acquired, from a position of unique and informed detachment, an intimate knowledge of the whole problem in practice.[1] At any rate—the Prague Government, the only dissentient, having been induced to acquiesce in secession—the issue was narrowed down to finding the means for an orderly execution of an agreed plan. That on such an issue the whole world should be plunged into war was the monstrous prospect that had to be contemplated until less than three days ago. It would inevitably have been realized if Herr Hitler had insisted on a spectacular "conquest" of the Sudetenland by German troops. The Czechs would certainly have resisted in arms, nor would any Power have had the right to attempt to dissuade them. France would have been drawn in by direct obligations to Czechoslovakia; Great Britain and the Soviet Union would have been certain to come to the help of France; and so the widening conflict would have involved all those peoples throughout the world who had watched with ever-increasing revulsion the development of brutal methods of national aggrandisement, and thought that the time had come to make a stand against them.

These methods have been publicly renounced by their principal exponents, to whom the peace-loving peoples should be ready to give full credit for their professions. But, at the moment when the

---

[1] Lord Runciman had been in Czechoslovakia in the summer of 1938 on a fact-finding and mediation meeting.

current racing towards the precipice seemed irresistible, it was the leadership of the British Prime Minister that showed how immense were the forces ranged on the side of reason against violence. The gathering urgency of persuasion was reinforced by unmistakable proofs of resolution for defence. France mobilized her army and manned her impregnable lines. Preparation in England, though slower in starting, as is the national habit, became at the crucial moment universal and formidable. The Fleet was mobilized; the anti-aircraft forces were brought into readiness; and civilians, taking post for emergency under voluntary as well as official schemes, showed plainly that the nation would not flinch. The Dominions were prompt to affirm their unanimity with the Mother Country. These things were not a threat, nor is it to be supposed that the German chancellor would yield to threats; but there is no doubt that the evidence that Mr. Chamberlain offered concession from strength and not from weakness won him a respect that might not otherwise have been accorded. Meanwhile other authoritive voices were uplifted for peace: the President of the United States spoke out for humanity, and the Italian Duce, responding to the Prime Minister's leadership, acknowledged that peace is a supreme interest to dictators as to other national rulers. Herr Hitler deferred, as no man need be ashamed of doing, to the protest of the whole world against war.

This was the crucial moment. That peace would follow the Munich negotiations was almost a foregone conclusion once a dictator had made the difficult renunciation of consenting to treat after he had announced his last word. The message so dramatically brought to Mr. Chamberlain in the House of Commons marked the true climax and ended the threat of war. In the upshot both sides have made concessions. Herr Hitler has yielded important points of substance, consenting, it seems, to modify in a number of places the new frontiers that claimed in the Godesberg memorandum. A dictator could hardly recede from the intention so loudly proclaimed of at least entering his new territories to-day; but the German troops will make a "token" entry and only move by defined stages, occupying several days, up to the limits agreed. By granting so much the Czechs suffer no practical loss, and they gain much by the acceptance of international control for the plebiscites that are to be held in areas of mixed race.

By the terms thus concluded the most dangerous threat of war in

Europe is at last removed, and by the joint declaration we are given the hope that others will be peacefully eliminated. That twofold achievement, by common consent, we owe first and foremost to the Prime Minister. Had the Government of the United Kingdom been in less resolute hands it is as certain as it can be that war, incalculable in its range, would have broken out against the wishes of every people concerned. The horror of such a catastrophe was not least in Germany. So much is clear from the immense popular enthusiasm with which Mr. Chamberlain was greeted on each of his three visits; a crowd of that disciplined nation does not break through a police cordon to acclaim a foreign statesman out of conventional politeness. Indeed these visits seem to have increased the Führer's understanding of his own people's sentiments, with a definite effect upon his policy. Let us hope that he may go on to see the wisdom of allowing them at all times to know the sentiments of other peoples instead of imposing between them a smoke-screen of ignorance and propaganda. For our own nation it remains to show our gratitude to Mr. Chamberlain, chiefly by learning the lessons taught by the great dangers through which we have been so finely led—that only a people prepared to face the worst can through their leaders cause peace to prevail in a crisis; but that the threat of ruin to civilization will recur unless injustices are faced and removed in quiet times, instead of being left to fester until it is too late for remedy. If these manifest truths, always recognized yet so seldom applied, are allowed to guide the diplomacy of the coming months, then we may at last expel from men's minds the deadly doctrine of preventive war and labour with confidence for a preventive peace.

LETTERS TO THE EDITOR

Then there were the letters to the editor, even more indicative, perhaps, of the public mood than the editorials. These three appeared in the London *Times* on the same day as the lead editorial just quoted:

"THERE'S A GOD UP THERE"

TO THE EDITOR OF THE TIMES

Sir,—Yesterday morning, that momentous September 28, I was sitting on a horse, a whipper-in some 20 yards ahead, his mount and himself a stiff note of interrogation. From the covert hard by hounds were stirring up the fox cubs, shrill squeaks of sheer excitement denoting the young entry on the trail of a rabbit. An old farmer, evidently past hard physical work, came up and we talked of foxes and their wiles.

Then he abruptly asked, "And what do you think of the position, Sir"? Before I could reply he half turned and pointed down to the Romney Marsh just below, where the mists were slowly dissipating into fine gauze filaments under the slanting rays of the new-risen sun. "On a Sunday evening, Sir, I have not time of week days, I comes through this field and sits at yonder point and looks down on the Marsh. Have done so for 40 years and more. Sometimes, when the sheep are nearly shorn, the light slants across and the bright green with the numbers of glistening white dots scattered over it is wonnerful beautiful. Is it all going to be spoilt, Sir?"

I looked down on the Marsh showing brilliant green patches where the mist had cleared and turned to look into those steady calm grey eyes. "No!" I said. "I have often looked at what you describe so well. No! I can't see it. I can't see that sky raining down death on this lovely countryside. I have tried to see it for the last few days. But I simply can't." He nodded gravely. "There's a God up there," pointing to the still misty heaven above the Marsh. "He will surely stop one man from committing so great a crime."

In that grey eye was faith and confidence. And the same amazing

Source: The Times, London, October 1, 1938.

stoical confidence has been exemplified during the past week on this countryside; and, not the least, amongst the women. These people are not likely to be stampeded.

And in the evening came the great news! And I thought of my talk at the dawning with my farmer friend. Was he surprised? I doubt it.

I am, Sir, your obedient servant,

E. P. STEBBING.

Romden, Smarden, Kent.

HOMAGE TO MR. CHAMBERLAIN

To The Editor of the Times

Sir,—The return of the Prime Minister brings to my mind certain ancient lines written of a very different man and with a very different moral to enforce:-

> Quid illo cive tulisset
> Natura in terris, quid Roma beatius unquam
> . . . .
> Cum de Teutonico vellet descendere curru? [1]

and the glory is none the less if there is no *agmen* of captives[2] or pomp of war to surround him.

Your obedient servant,

RANKEILLOUR.

[1] "What could Nature, what could Rome,
Have ever produced in the world more blessed with glory than
That citizen if he had breathed his great soul out as he,
After marching captive troops in the full pomp of victory
Was about to step from his German chariot?"
The passage—a reference to Marius' triumph over the Cimbri and Teutones in 102 B.C.—is from Juvenal's *Satires* (Vol. X, pp. 278–282, in the Creekmore translation).
[2] Mass of captives.

TO THE EDITOR OF THE TIMES

Sir,—On all sides one hears nothing but praise for Mr. Chamberlain's great personal efforts entailing strenuous endurance, and a way should be found of showing appreciation of his patriotic work in some tangible form in which every one could join.

Would it be possible for the Government to print 2,000,000 souvenir stamps of a face value of sixpence each which could be on sale at all post offices for one month?

The £50,000 realized could be handed to the Prime Minister to create some lasting remembrance as a small expression of gratitude from the masses; the public would have a small memento of this historic event; and, if the idea is acceptable, I should be pleased to meet the cost of printing.

Yours very truly,

E. W. MEYERSTEIN.

Morants Court, Dunton Green, Kent, September 29.

CHAPTER THREE

A New Response: Prague to War in Poland

TWO EDITORIALS

No souvenir stamps were issued. Perhaps they should have been, for the mood of Munich would evaporate very quickly. The Sudeten Germans had been a means to an end; as far as his foreign aims were concerned, Hitler had no more come to the last of his demands than he had after the Austrian *Anschluss.* In March 1939, he startled the appeasers with his next move. At the obviously forced request of the president of the surviving Czechoslovak state, German troops moved into the country. The Czech part, under its old Habsburg names of Bohemia and Moravia, was declared a German protectorate, while the Slovak part received nominal independence. With Hitler ("we want no Czechs") riding into Prague as a conqueror a mere six months after Munich, the premises of appeasement no longer held. Two editorials in the London *Times* signaled the change in Britain's mood. The first appeared on March 16, 1939, the day after the German action, the second on March 17.

MILITARISM IN ACTION

Hitherto in each of three successive German coups—the Rhineland, Austria, Sudetenland—though the method has been brutal and overbearing, it has been difficult not to allow some extenuation for it in Allied blunders of the past and not to see in it some substance of justice. Possibly a plausible defence might have been made even of German action in Slovakia. . . . But no defence of any kind, no pretext of the slightest plausibility, can be offered for the violent extinction of Czech independence in the historic Czech homelands of Bohemia and Moravia. On the contrary it violates a whole succession of solemn pledges given by the German Führer himself.

For the first time since Nazism came to power German policy has moved unequivocally and deliberately into the open. . . .

. . . Everywhere confidence is set back. The boon which even a sure modicum of good faith and agreement could shower upon the hard pressed peoples of Europe is once more postponed. The Western world increases its vigilance and its solidity, not less but more determined that within its own wide sphere there shall be no weakness in face of force or the threat of force.

Source: The Times, London, March 16 and 17, 1939.

THE NEW PROTECTORATE

One solitary gain from this miserable business has been that the methods of Nazism have now been more clearly than ever before revealed in all their cunning and ruthlessness. . . .

. . . The feeling is now universal that it is no longer possible to place confidence in the word of the Nazi Government, and that even principles which have the sanction of many years of Nazi preaching and practice may be cast aside at once if they happen to be inconvenient. . . . The purpose of Nazi policy is more and more revealed as sheer aggrandisement—the brutal domination of other countries for the sole purpose of increasing the power of the Reich. . . .

2.   NEVILLE CHAMBERLAIN

"VALUE FREEDOM MORE"

On the day the second editorial appeared, Neville Chamberlain spoke in Birmingham to defend his policies, but also to add that German policy seemed to have entered a new phase—"public opinion in the world has received a sharper shock than has even yet been administered to it"—and that the West would have to reassess its policies. It was a relatively mild speech still; the door to understanding was not to be closed entirely. Still, he concluded by saying:

It is only six weeks ago that I was speaking in this city, and that I alluded to rumours and suspicions which I said ought to be swept away. I pointed out that any demand to dominate the world by force was one which the democracies must resist, and I added that I could not believe that such a challenge was intended because no Government with the interests of its own people at heart could expose them for such a claim to the horrors of world war.

Source: Chamberlain, *In Search of Peace*, p. 275.

And indeed, with the lessons of history for all to read, it seems incredible that we should see such a challenge. I feel bound to repeat that, while I am not prepared to engage this country by new unspecified commitments operating under conditions which cannot now be foreseen, yet no greater mistake could be made than to suppose that, because it believes war to be a senseless and cruel thing, this nation has so lost its fibre that it will not take part to the utmost of its power resisting such a challenge if it ever were made. For that declaration I am convinced that I have not merely the support, the sympathy, the confidence of my fellow-countrymen and countrywomen, but I shall have also the approval of the whole British Empire and of all other nations who value peace indeed, but who value freedom even more.

3.   BRITISH FOREIGN OFFICE

CORRESPONDENCE

Actually, Chamberlain did have some new commitments in mind. The next direction toward which the Germans might move was thought to be either Rumania, with its oil resources, or, and this seemed even more likely, Poland, whose German minority offered as convenient an excuse for aggression as Czechoslovakia's had. What the British proposed now was a three power guarantee of Poland, but this proved difficult, since the Poles were nearly as afraid of Soviet aid as they were of German aggression. The diplomatic files tell the story of Britain's diplomatic efforts in the days that followed Prague:

Source: Documents on British Foreign Policy 1919–1939, Vol. IV, pp. 291, 400, 402–403, 515–517, 540.

VISCOUNT HALIFAX TO SIR N. HENDERSON (BERLIN)[1]

No. 68 Telegraphic
FOREIGN OFFICE, March 17, 1939,
8.50 p.m.

Please inform German Government that His Majesty's Government desire to make it plain to them that they cannot but regard the events of the past few days as a complete repudiation of the Munich Agreement and a denial of the spirit in which the negotiators of that Agreement bound themselves to co-operate for a peaceful settlement.

His Majesty's Government must also take this occasion to protest against the changes effected in Czecho-Slovakia by German military action, which are in their view devoid of any basis of legality.

VISCOUNT HALIFAX TO SIR E. PHIPPS (PARIS),
SIR W. SEEDS (MOSCOW),
AND SIR H. KENNARD (WARSAW)

No. 94 Telegraphic
FOREIGN OFFICE, March 20, 1939,
11.5 p.m.

1. In spite of doubts as to accuracy of reports of German ultimatum to Roumania, recent German absorption of Czecho-Slovakia shows clearly that German Government are resolved to go beyond their hitherto avowed aim of consolidation of German race. They have now extended their conquest to another nation and if this should prove to be part of a definite policy of domination there is no State in Europe which is not directly or ultimately threatened.

2. In the circumstances thus created it seems to His Majesty's Government in the United Kingdom to be desirable to proceed without delay to the organisation of mutual support on the part of all those who realise the necessity of protecting international society from further violation of fundamental laws on which it rests.

[1] Lord Halifax was Britain's foreign secretary, Sir Nevile Henderson, the ambassador to Berlin.

3. As a first step they propose that the French, Soviet and Polish Governments should join with His Majesty's Government in signing and publishing a formal Declaration the terms of which they suggest should be on the lines of the following:-

'We the undersigned, duly authorised to that effect, hereby declare that, inasmuch as peace and security in Europe are matters of common interest and concern, and since European peace and security may be affected by any action which constitutes a threat to the political independence of any European State, our respective Governments hereby undertake immediately to consult together as to what steps should be taken to offer joint resistance to any such action.'

4. It appears to us that the publication of such a Declaration would in itself be a valuable contribution to the stability of Europe and we should propose that publication should be followed by an examination by the signatories of any specific situation which requires it, with a view to determining the nature of any action which might be taken.

5. Please endeavour immediately to obtain the views of Government to which you are accredited. His Majesty's Government would be prepared to sign Declaration immediately the three other Governments indicate their readiness to do so.

6. We should propose to say nothing of this to the other Governments concerned before the four Powers are agreed on the Declaration.

LETTER FROM MR. CHAMBERLAIN TO SIGNOR MUSSOLINI

10 DOWNING STREET, March 20, 1939

Dear Signor Mussolini,

Last September I made an appeal to you to which you responded at once. As a result peace was preserved, to the relief of the whole world.

In the critical situation which has arisen from the events of last week, I feel impelled to address you again. You will remember that, in the course of that visit to Rome last January which I shall always recollect with deep satisfaction and pleasure, you asked me whether I had any points which I wished to raise with you. I replied that there was one which was causing me considerable anxiety. I had heard many rumours that Herr Hitler was planning some new *coup,* and I knew that he was pushing forward his armament production though I could see no quarter from which he was in the slightest danger of attack. You then expressed the opinion that Herr Hitler wanted peace in which to fuse together the Greater Reich, and that you did not believe that he had any new adventure in mind.

Whatever may have been his intentions then, he has in fact carried out a measure which appears to be in complete contradiction to the assurances he gave me. You will have noted from my speech of the 17th of this month the view that I take of this new and most disturbing move, which has created the most profound resentment in this country and elsewhere.

What above all has impressed everyone here is the implication of this departure from the principles laid down previously by the German Government inasmuch as for the first time they have incorporated in the Reich a large non-German population. Does this mean that the events in Czecho-Slovakia are only the prelude to further attempts at control of other States?

If it does I foresee that sooner or later, and probably sooner, another major war is inevitable. It is inconceivable that any country should want such a war, but if the alternative before the other States of Europe is that one by one they are to be dominated by force they will assuredly prefer to fight for their liberties.

You will I know realise that I do not seek to interfere with the Rome-Berlin Axis. I fully understand that that is regarded as a fixed part of your foreign policy. But I have always believed that peace could be established provided that no one power was determined to dominate all the others. What has now happened has raised the gravest doubts as to whether this condition is present. Fresh moves in the same direction would turn those doubts into certainties.

You told me that your policy was one of peace and that you would at any time be willing to use your influence in that direction. I earnestly hope that you may feel it possible, in any way that may be open to you, to take such action in these anxious days as may allay present tension and do something to restore the confidence that has been shattered.

Believe me,
Yours sincerely,
NEVILLE CHAMBERLAIN

VISCOUNT HALIFAX TO SIR H. KENNARD (WARSAW)
AND SIR R. HOARE (BUCHAREST)

No. 56 Telegraphic
FOREIGN OFFICE, March 27, 1939, 11.30 p.m.

(No action should be taken on the present telegram pending further instructions.)

1. My enquiries in the various capitals concerned have shown that it will not be possible to proceed without modification with the proposed Four-Power Declaration. While the French Government have accepted the proposal, and while the Soviet Government have accepted, subject to acceptance by France and Poland, the Polish Government are reluctant, for reasons which I appreciate, to associate themselves with the Soviet Union in a public declaration of this kind.

2. His Majesty's Government have been in close and confidential consultation with the Polish Government on this subject, and although possible variants of the original scheme have been discussed, it is becoming clear that our attempts to consolidate the situation will be frustrated if the Soviet Union is openly associated with the initiation of the scheme. Recent telegrams from a number of His Majesty's Missions abroad have warned us that the inclusion of Russia would not only jeopardise the success of our constructive effort, but also tend to consolidate the relations of the parties to the Anti-Comintern Pact, as well as excite anxiety among a number of friendly Governments.

3. It is evident, therefore, that some alternative method of approach must be sought. In any scheme, the inclusion of Poland is vital as the one strong Power bordering on Germany in the East, and the inclusion of Roumania is also of the first importance, since Roumania may be the State primarily menaced by Germany's plans for Eastern expansion.

4. His Majesty's Government have, therefore, decided to make an approach to the Polish and Roumanian Governments in the following sense. The French Government have agreed to make a corresponding approach.

(*a*) Germany may either directly attack Poland or Roumania, or may undermine either country's independence, whether by processes of economic penetration or national disintegration, as in the case of Czecho-Slovakia, or by indirect military pressure, which, in the case of Roumania, might take the form of Hungarian troop concentrations. Are Poland and Roumania respectively prepared actively to resist if their own independence is threatened in any of these ways?

(*b*) If so, Great Britain and France would be prepared to come to the help of the threatened State. It would be understood that, as a counterpart for the undertaking by Great Britain and France to support Poland and Roumania, Poland and Roumania would keep Great Britain and France fully and promptly informed of any developments threatening their independence;

(*c*) The assurance offered in (*b*) is dependent upon Poland coming to the help of Roumania, if the latter is the State threatened. We should wish to know whether Roumania would be prepared to come to the help of Poland if the latter were the State threatened.

(*d*) (The present section (*d*) of the communication is to be made to the Polish Government only since Poland, unlike Roumania, has a Treaty of Mutual Assistance with France, and is a stronger military power than Roumania.) The undertaking given by Great Britain and France[1] under (*b*) would be given as part of a reciprocal arrangement by which if Great Britain or France were attacked by Germany, or if they went to war with Germany to resist German aggression anywhere in Western Europe or Yugoslavia, Poland would come to their help.

5. If the position of Poland and Roumania can be consolidated, Turkey and Greece could more easily be rallied to the common cause and would be more likely to be able to make an effective contritution.

6. It is important that the Polish and Roumanian Governments should be made aware of the manner in which we would propose to deal with the Soviet difficulty. It is desirable to preserve the interest of the Soviet Union in this scheme. The intention would be, at some convenient moment in the discussions, to explain to the Soviet Government that it was proposed in the first place to proceed with the Governments of the two countries nearer to Germany and most likely to be affected by the potential danger of the situation. In the

[1] A telegram sent two days later asked that the words "to Poland" be inserted at this point.

event of an attack on Poland or Roumania there would be good reasons on the merits of the case for trying to secure some measure of Soviet participation. I believe that even the benevolent neutrality of the Soviet Union would be to the advantage of these two countries in case of war, and that they might indeed be grateful in an emergency to have at their disposal such war material as Soviet industry would be in a position to furnish. I am disposed in the first place to ascertain the view of the Soviet Government as to their likely attitude to this proposal. It is important nøt to reinforce their tendency towards isolation and I propose to consider in due course how best to retain their close interest which is, after all, to their own general advantage.

7. It is essential of course that the present approach to the Polish and Roumanian Governments should be kept secret, as well as any negotiations that may follow it. Once, however, agreement had been secured, it would be necessary, for constitutional reasons, that some statement should be made in Parliament. His Majesty's Government would at any rate have to state in public the assurances which they had given to the Polish and Roumanian Governments. It is possible that the Polish Government might be reluctant to agree to make public such counter-assurances as they would have given to us, but His Majesty's Government would certainly be pressed to say whether any such counter-assurances had been given and they would very much hope to be in a position to announce the fact.

8. Your French colleague will receive similar instructions and you should, after consulting him, speak to the Minister for Foreign Affairs in the sense of the present telegram. You should not leave with him any statement in writing.

Repeated to Paris and Moscow.

SIR E. PHIPPS (PARIS) TO VISCOUNT HALIFAX
(RECEIVED MARCH 29, 5.50 p.m.)

No. 136 Telegraphic
PARIS, March 29, 1939, 4.25 p.m.

Your telegram No. 56 to Warsaw.
French Government agree.
Repeated to Bucharest, Moscow and Warsaw.

NEVILLE CHAMBERLAIN

A GUARANTEE TO POLAND

The result was that only Britain and France guaranteed Poland's integrity, but their statement of intent, when Chamberlain next spoke in Parliament on March 31, 1938, was all the more unambiguous:

The right hon. Gentleman the Leader of the Opposition (Mr. Attlee) asked me this morning whether I could make a statement as to the European situation. As I said this morning, His Majesty's Government have no official confirmation of the rumours of any projected attack on Poland and they must not, therefore, be taken as accepting them as true.

I am glad to take this opportunity of stating again the general policy of His Majesty's Government. They have constantly advocated the adjustment, by way of free negotiation between the parties concerned, of any differences that may arise between them. They consider that this is the natural and proper course where differences exist. In their opinion there should be no question incapable of solution by peaceful means, and they would see no justification for the substitution of force or threats of force for the method of negotiation.

As the House is aware, certain consultations are now proceeding with other Governments. In order to make perfectly clear the position of His Majesty's Government in the meantime before those consultations are concluded, I now have to inform the House that during that period, in the event of any action which clearly threatened Polish independence, and which the Polish Government accordingly considered it vital to resist with their national forces, His Majesty's Government would feel themselves bound at once to lend the Polish Government all support in their power. They have given the Polish Government an assurance to this effect.

I may add that the French Government have authorised me to make it plain that they stand in the same position in this matter as do His Majesty's Government.

Source: Chamberlain, *In Search of Peace*, p. 279.

5.

ERICH KORDT

HITLER'S ESTIMATE OF GREAT BRITAIN

Yet Hitler chose not to believe the new Chamberlain. A high German foreign ministry official, Erich Kordt, writing soon after the war, remembered the Führer's reaction:

. . . Neither during the Rhineland occupation nor during the Spanish Civil War, no more than during the Austrian Anschluss, did Hitler believe that the British would intervene. He had convinced himself, too, that Britain would never have gone to war for Czechoslovakia, either, no matter what the circumstances. Now, he was no more ready to take the British alliance with Poland any more seriously than London's statements during the Abyssinian war. "The British are bluffing," was his constant answer to warning voices. In order to be rid of such bothersome opinions, Ribbentrop[1] forbade anyone's saying that Britain might take part in a war. Whoever spoke or even thought that way, he said, was in the pay, or at any rate under the influence, of the British Secret Service. . . .

6.

PROPAGANDA MINISTRY

PRESS DIRECTIVES

That Hitler was determined to go ahead with his Polish plans was apparent from the controlled German press. Both the Munich and the Prague crisis had been preceded by organized German press campaigns. In the

Source: Erich Kordt, *Wahn und Wirklichkeit* (Union Deutsche Verlagsgesellschaft, Stuttgart, 1948), p. 168 (translated by the editor).
[1] Hitler's foreign minister since 1938.
Source: *Zeitschriften-Dienst*, No. 421 (July 15, 1939), p. 3; and No. 640 (August 26, 1939), p. 7 (translated by the editor).

summer of 1939, the public attacks on Poland began. They were fairly subtle at first, but soon became more massive. These instructions, issued by Goebbels' Propaganda Ministry to the German periodical press, which all German publications were obliged to follow, tell much of the story.

[July 15, 1939:]

General Tendency: Prepare material, and as circumstances require, publish.

Emphasize: Poland's political crisis a permanent state of affairs; Poland the eternal sick man; a state that always collapses. Poland's main problem: the minority issue. Old Poland neither a nation nor a state, but rather the negation of both.

Avoid: Attacks on present-day Poland or on current conditions, references to current political intentions or immediate policies.

THEMES AND SUGGESTIONS:

Political: Poland under German protection for 300 years. From 963 to the thirteenth century Poland almost uninterruptedly a German fief; Poland's king a vassal of the German emperor. Advantages for Poland's development. Polish unreason attempts to undo ties with Germany. . . .

[August 29, 1939:]

POLAND THREATENS THE PEACE OF EUROPE

Why Topical? Unbearable Polish methods toward ethnic Germans. Democratic press stubbornly suppresses all expressions of Polish hatred and megalomania.

Aim: Make apparent to the world Poland's love of aggression, concept of "Polish powder keg." Make foreign opinion realize the unbearable threat of war which is an intrinsic part of Polish chauvinism.

GENERAL TENDENCY:

Emphasize: Uncontrollable Polish temper. For years, Polish megalomania whipped up to boiling point. Government increasingly losing control. Poland driving Europe into war for the sake of its imperialist aims. . . .

7.   GEORGE F. KENNAN

THE NONAGGRESSION PACT

Yet Hitler's mind, in the summer of 1939, was not entirely made up. He wanted war with Poland, but not with England. The solution that occurred to him was to come to terms with his arch-enemy, the Soviet Union. For without Russia's assistance there was little that the West could do to help Poland. George Kennan, who knew both the Germans and the Russians well as a result of his diplomatic service in Berlin and Moscow, and who at the time was secretary of legation at Prague, has described the making of the Nazi-Soviet pact.

After Munich, events took a rapid and dramatic course. Hitler, instead of being directed onto the paths of peace, was irritated and disturbed by the reaction to Munich in the West, particularly by the signs of a growing realization on the part of the Western governments that it was high time they rearmed. He had no intention whatsoever of foregoing the remainder of his program: the demands on Poland, Memel, and Danzig. Yet the sharp reaction to Munich in the West implied the danger that London and Paris might not be prepared to take any more of this lying down. The beginnings of the French and British rearmament effort meant that time was running out on him. This presented him with a difficult problem of policy.

Source: George F. Kennan, *Russia and the West Under Lenin and Stalin* (Little, Brown and Co., Boston, 1960), Ch. 21, "The Nonaggression Pact," pp. 324–329.

For some weeks at the outset of 1939 Hitler appears to have toyed with the possibility of inducing the Poles to agree to the peaceful incorporation of Danzig into the Reich, and to the cutting of the Polish Corridor by a new German corridor across it. But the Poles, in a series of conversations conducted in January 1939, resisted these approaches. Furious at this recalcitrance, which cut off his easiest and most favorable prospects, Hitler made his first major mistake. He proceeded, in March 1939, to occupy all of what was left of Czechoslovakia, except the easternmost province of Ruthenia, which he tossed contemptuously to the Hungarians. He had delayed this move, which was bound to frighten the Poles, so long as there was a chance that Poland would give him what he wanted by peaceful agreement. Since the Poles proved obdurate, he petulantly went ahead to extinguish what was left of the Czechoslovak state.

By this move, Hitler placed himself on Poland's southern flank, and improved, of course, his position for further pressure against the Poles. But this represented a flagrant violation of the assurances he had given to the British at Munich; and it forced people in London and Paris to realize that even the ultimate act of appeasement involved in the Munich settlement had been a failure—that Hitler could not safely be permitted to gain any more bloodless victories. The British reacted by summoning the Polish Foreign Minister, Josef Beck, to London for negotiations, and by proclaiming a British guarantee of the integrity of the territory of Poland. Together with the French, they also entered into negotiations with the Soviet government to see whether a real and effective alliance against Hitler could not at last be brought into being. These negotiations, which began in the middle of April 1939, were pursued in Moscow throughout the summer.

All this put Hitler in a difficult box. As things now stood, he could not gain his objectives without an attack on Poland. He was obliged to recognize that he could not attack Poland, in the face of the British guarantee, without risk of involving himself in a war with France and Britain. For a time, he thought of attacking England and France first, letting Poland go until later. But even this he could not risk if there was any possibility that France and England might be joined by Russia. Russia had, therefore, to be neutralized. It had to be neutralized whatever he did, whether he attacked Poland first or England and France. This meant that the

Soviet negotiations with the French and British in Moscow had somehow to be spiked. If they could be spiked, perhaps this would not only keep Russia out of the conflict but England and France would then not dare to fight at all. How could this be done? Only by a deal with Stalin.

Hitler viewed only with deepest distaste and suspicion the prospect of negotiating with the Russians. While he personally admired Stalin, he was sincere in his loathing for Russian Communism. For some weeks, from mid-May to early July, while permitting lower-level German representatives to take soundings of various sorts with their opposite Soviet numbers, Hitler wrestled with this problem. For a time he appears to have toyed, as an alternative, with the idea of contenting himself for the moment with a bloodless seizure of Danzig alone.

Stalin, meanwhile, sensing the approach of the final crisis, convinced that Hitler was going to strike somewhere, and determined to purchase his own safety, played his cards with consummate skill. To the Germans he made absolutely clear his willingness to discuss a deal. On March 10, 1939, even before the German occupation of Bohemia and Moravia, he had said, in a celebrated speech to the Eighteenth Party Congress in Moscow, that Russia did not propose to pull anybody else's chestnuts out of the fire for them. This was another way of saying that Russia was not going to fight Britain's or France's battles—that she would look after herself in her own way. A clearer hint to the Germans could scarcely have been devised. The Germans indicated that they understood and were interested. Six weeks later, Stalin removed Litvinov as foreign minister and turned the job over to Molotov. This was the first time since 1918 that the Foreign Affairs Ministry had been given to a member of the Politbureau. The change demonstrated that Stalin was preparing for major moves of foreign policy. At the same time, he continued to draw out the negotiations with the French and British, in order to have a second string to his bow and as a means of frightening the Germans into agreement.

For some reason—perhaps because he had become convinced that the Russians were serious in their desire for a deal, perhaps because the Poles had made it evident that they would regard even a bloodless seizure of Danzig as a *casus belli*—but certainly in any case, with the knowledge that the season was advancing and military decisions could no longer be postponed, Hitler, in early

July, stopped his hesitation and made up his mind to attack Poland. Secret orders were at once issued to the armed forces to be prepared to launch the attack at the end of August. The all-clear signal was given, for the first time, for intensive, far-reaching negotiations with the Soviet government.

From now on, it was high politics, in the most dramatic and sinister sense of the term. On July 26, in the private dining room of a Berlin restaurant, Russian and German representatives got down to brass tacks. It was hinted to the Russians that Germany would be prepared to pay for Soviet neutrality, in the event of a German-Polish war, by turning over to the Soviet Union considerable areas of eastern Europe. Armed with this secret knowledge, Stalin and Molotov increased the pressure on the unsuspecting British and French negotiators in Moscow. In veiled terms the question was put to the French and British: would *they*, in the event of a war, be prepared to place large sections of eastern Europe at the mercy of Russia? Would *they*, for example, consent to regard Moscow as the guarantor of the three Baltic States, and entitled to do what it wanted there? And would *they* compel the Poles and Rumanians to accept Soviet troops on their territory in the event of an action against Germany?

You can see what was going on. Stalin, with both sides competing for his favor, was trying to find out who was the highest bidder. Of the two bidders, only one, the Germans, knew that the other side was bidding; the other bidder seems to have had no knowledge that any other bid was being made. Faced with these demands, the French and British temporized. They wanted Russian help against Germany, but they did not feel that they could buy it at the price of the sacrifice of their Polish allies or of the Baltic States. The Germans, of course, had no such inhibitions. Hitler, calculating out of his own infinite cynicism and opportunism, figured that he could always handle the Russians later; if he could be sure of getting his half of Poland now, and getting it without great danger of a world war, let the Russians, for the moment, have the rest, and certain other parts of eastern Europe in the bargain.

Seeing that the Russians were inclining in this direction, and with his own military deadline for the attack on Poland crowding in on him, Hitler decided to force the issue. On August 15 the Soviet government was informed that the Germans were prepared to send their foreign minister, Ribbentrop, to Moscow in the near future, "to lay the foundations for a definite improvement in German-Soviet relations." This meant that the Germans were willing to do business on the basis discussed in the secret talks. The next day another message arrived asking that the date of Ribbentrop's arrival be advanced to August 12, only two days hence, on the grounds that

> . . . in view of the present situation, and of the possibility of the occurrence any day of serious incidents . . , a basic and rapid clarification of German-Russian relations and the mutual adjustment of the present questions are desirable.

This meant that the German attack on Poland was only a matter of days.

The moment of decision for Stalin had now arrived. The Japanese had again been acting up. Major hostilities involving, in fact, several divisions—tanks, artillery, aircraft, the entire paraphernalia of war—were just then in progress on the Mongolian frontier. The British and French negotiators, still in Moscow, suspected nothing. If Stalin turned down the German offer, he would of course have to come to some agreement with the British and French; he could not leave himself in a position of complete isolation in the face of the German attack on Poland. But he could then expect no mercy at the hands of Hitler; and if the British and French failed to engage Hitler's force in the West, Russia would be confronted at last by that war for which she was so ill-prepared: a war on two fronts, against both Germany and Japan. He would have to accept combat, furthermore, along the existing western Soviet frontiers, uncomfortably near to both the great cities of Leningrad and Moscow. If, on the other hand, he accepted Hitler's offer, he could not only remain aloof initially from the impending German-Polish conflict, with the possibility that Hitler might even become involved with the French and British, but he would be permitted, in the bargain, to take over a large area of eastern Europe. He could use this as a buffer zone in case Hitler attacked him at a later date. Meanwhile, the acquisition of it would be a great boon to his prestige.

To Stalin a bird in the hand was worth two in the bush. He chose, as he had perhaps secretly known all along that he would choose if he had the opportunity, for Hitler. The answer was given to send Ribbentrop along.

The Germans were mad with elation over the Soviet answer. They interpreted the negotiations which the French and British had been conducting so openly all summer with the Soviet government to mean that Britain and France, unless assured of Russian help, would never dare to oppose a German attack on Poland. Soviet acceptance of Ribbentrop's visit excluded even the possibility of the British and French going to war. Hitler it seemed had played, this time, for the highest stakes and had won. The last of his great objectives was about to be achieved; and it would be achieved, like the others, without bringing about the world war which the pessimists had always warned would be the result of his adventures.

You know the rest. On August 23, Ribbentrop flew to Moscow for twenty-four hours of hectic negotiation. That night, the German-Soviet Nonaggression Pact was signed. Its publication burst on the unsuspecting world like a bombshell, throwing consternation into the Western chanceries, bewilderment into the ranks of the Western liberal friends of the Soviet Union, and utter chaos into the foreign Communist parties which for six years, at Moscow's direction, had been following the most violent possible anti-Nazi line and denouncing anyone who as much as said a civil word in Hitler's direction.

Both sides, in signing this pact, were aware that it sealed the fate of Poland, that war—a German-Polish war, that is—would be only a matter of days. . . .

8.

TREATY OF NONAGGRESSION BETWEEN GERMANY AND THE UNION OF SOVIET SOCIALIST REPUBLICS

This was the wording of the public part of the Nazi-Soviet pact:

The Government of the German Reich and the Government of the Union of Soviet Socialist Republics desirous of strengthening the cause of peace between Germany and the U.S.S.R., and proceeding from the fundamental provisions of the Neutrality Agreement concluded in April 1926 between Germany and the U.S.S.R., have reached the following agreement:

ARTICLE I

Both High Contracting Parties obligate themselves to desist from any act of violence, any aggressive action, and any attack on each other, either individually or jointly with other powers.

ARTICLE II

Should one of the High Contracting Parties become the object of belligerent action by a third power; the other High Contracting Party shall in no manner lend its support to this third power.

ARTICLE III

The Governments of the two High Contracting Parties shall in the future maintain continual contact with one another for the purpose of consultation in order to exchange information on problems affecting their common interests.

Source: Raymond J. Sontag and James Stuart Beddie, eds., *Nazi-Soviet Relations 1939–1941, Documents from the Archives of the German Foreign Office* (Department of State, Washington, D.C., 1948).

ARTICLE IV

Neither of the two High Contracting Parties shall participate in any grouping of powers whatsoever that is directly or indirectly aimed at the other party.

ARTICLE V

Should disputes or conflicts arise between the High Contracting Parties over problems of one kind or another, both parties shall settle these disputes or conflicts exclusively through friendly exchange of opinion or, if necessary, through the establishment of arbitration commissions.

ARTICLE VI

The present treaty is concluded for a period of ten years, with the proviso that, in so far as one of the High Contracting Parties does not denounce it one year prior to the expiration of this period, the validity of this treaty shall automatically be extended for another five years.

ARTICLE VII

The present treaty shall be ratified within the shortest possible time. The ratifications shall be exchanged in Berlin. The agreement shall enter into force as soon as it is signed.

Done in duplicate, in the German and Russian languages.

Moscow, August 23, 1939.

For the Government   With full power of the
of the German Reich: Government of the U.S.S.R.:
V. RIBBENTROP   V. MOLOTOV

9.

A PRESS INTERVIEW

Explaining the pact was not altogether easy for two regimes that until then had been the most bitter and vociferous enemies. But the propaganda machines made the necessary adjustments. In the German case, Nazi propaganda now hinted at a certain affinity between the two ideologies in that they both despised "plutocracy"; besides, of course, there were the strategic uses of the pact that did not even need to be hinted at. In the Russian case, the explanation was that the Soviet government had had practically no alternative but to come to terms with the Germans, since Britain and France had been so reluctant in their negotiations with Moscow, and since, even more important, the Poles themselves had barred any Russian aid. The case was stated among others, by General Voroshilov at the end of August 1939.

Q. What was the outcome of the negotiations with the British and French military missions?

A. Since serious differences were revealed the negotiations were discontinued. The military missions have left Moscow.

Q. May we know the nature of these differences?

A. The Soviet military mission thought that the USSR, having no common frontier with the aggressor, could come to the help of France, England, or Poland only if its troops were allowed to pass through Polish territory, for there is no other way to come into contact with the troops of the aggressor. Just as the English and American troops in the last world war could not have taken part in military co-operation with the armed forces of France if they had not been able to operate on French territory, so Soviet armed forces could not take part in military co-operation with the armed forces of France and England if they were not admitted into Polish territory.

Despite the fact that this attitude was completely and obviously correct, the French and British Military Missions did not agree with the Soviet mission. In addition, the Polish Government openly stated that it did not need and would not accept military aid from the USSR.

This circumstance made military co-operation between the USSR and these countries impossible.

Source: Pravda, August 27, 1939 (translated by Horst Lorscheider and Edward Roveto).

This was the basis of the disagreement. It was on this that negotiations were broken off.

Q. Was anything said during the negotiations about help to Poland by means of raw materials and military materials?

A. No, nothing. Help by means of raw materials and military equipment is a business matter, and no pact of mutual assistance, still less any military convention, is required to give Poland raw materials and military equipment. The United States, like a number of other countries, has concluded no mutual assistance pact or military convention with Japan, but for two years they have been selling raw materials and war materials to the Japanese, although Japan is in a state of war with China. During the negotiations we discussed help not by way of raw materials and military equipment, but by way of troops.

Q. The diplomatic correspondent of the *Daily Herald* writes that the English and French military missions asked the Soviet mission whether the USSR was ready to supply Poland with aircraft and military supplies, and to hold the Red Army in readiness on the frontier, and that the Soviet military mission answered that immediately on the outbreak of war Vilna and Novogrudok on the north-east would be occupied, and the Lvov, Tarnopol, and Stanislavsky districts on the south-east; that from these positions the Red Army could give military help to the Poles, if that should be required.

Do you think this statement of the *Daily Herald* diplomatic correspondent in accordance with the facts or not?

A. The statement is a lie from beginning to end, its author an impudent liar, and the paper which publishes this lying statement a libellous paper.

Q. Reuters reports by wireless: Today Voroshilov told the heads of the British and French missions that in view of the conclusion of the non-aggression treaty between the USSR and Germany, the Soviet Government considers further negotiations with England and France pointless.

Is this in accordance with the facts or not?

A. No, it is not. Military negotiations with England and France were not broken off because the USSR concluded a non-aggression pact with Germany; on the contrary, the USSR concluded a non-aggression pact with Germany as a result, *inter alia,* of the fact that the military negotiations with France and England had reached a deadlock because of insuperable difficulties.

10.

SECRET ADDITIONAL PROTOCOL TO THE TREATY OF NONAGGRESSION BETWEEN GERMANY AND THE UNION OF SOVIET SOCIALIST REPUBLICS

Despite its tone, the argument was not without merit. It did omit an essential fact, however. This was that Hitler had promised Stalin half of Poland in return for his neutrality, and a major (and clearly delineated) sphere of influence in northern and southeastern Europe as well. The published part of the Nazi-Soviet pact was accompanied by a secret one, which read:

On the occasion of the signature of the Nonaggression Pact between the German Reich and the Union of Socialist Soviet Republics the undersigned plenipotentiaries of each of the two parties discussed in strictly confidential conversations the question of the boundary of their respective spheres of influence in Eastern Europe. These conversations led to the following conclusions:

1. In the event of a territorial and political rearrangement in the areas belonging to the Baltic States (Finland, Estonia, Latvia, Lithuania), the northern boundary of Lithuania shall represent the boundary of the spheres of influence of Germany and the U.S.S.R. In this connection the interest of Lithuania in the Vilna area is recognized by each party.

2. In the event of a territorial and political rearrangement of the areas belonging to the Polish state the spheres of influence of Germany and the U.S.S.R. shall be bounded approximately by the line of the rivers Narew, Vistula, and San.

The question of whether the interests of both parties make desirable the maintenance of an independent Polish state and how such a state should be bounded can only be definitely determined in the course of further political developments.

In any event both Governments will resolve this question by means of a friendly agreement.

Source: Sontag and Beddie, eds., *Nazi-Soviet Relations*, p. 78.

3. With regard to Southeastern Europe attention is called by the Soviet side to its interest in Bessarabia. The German side declares its complete political disinterestedness in these areas.

4. This protocol shall be treated by both parties as strictly secret.

MOSCOW, August 23, 1939.

For the Government of the German Reich:	Plenipotentiary of the Government of the U.S.S.R.:
V. RIBBENTROP	V. MOLOTOV

11.   PROPAGANDA MINISTRY

PRESS DIRECTIVES

A little over a week after the signing of the pact, Hitler attacked Poland. Even now, however, he tried to prevent a wider war (which he might lose). "Everything that I undertake is directed against Russia," he told a neutral intermediary, who could be expected to convey that message to London. Poland was a mere means to an end. He hoped that the West was not "too stupid and too blind to grasp this." But no matter what the Western powers should do, he was ready to act, and on September 1, 1939, German troops crossed into Poland. They did so without a formal declaration of war, and another directive from Goebbels' ministry explains why. It is a document that, for all its brevity, forecasts much of the future, suggesting both the role that propaganda would play in the war and the ominous fate that awaited Poland.

ADDITIONAL INSTRUCTION
OF THE REICH MINISTRY
FOR POPULAR ENLIGHTENMENT AND PROPAGANDA

1. In no connection is the word, or the concept, *war* to be used in any of the periodical press, since we are merely driving back Polish attacks.

Source: Zeitschriften-Dienst, Special Insert, Nos. 718–20 (September 1, 1939), n.p. (translated by the editor).

2. The speech of the Führer to the Reichstag (September 1, 1939) is to be made the basis of discussion of the current situation. . . .

3. In *no* case may any plans or predictions regarding Poland's future, etc., be discussed.

12.   PAUL SCHMIDT

EXTRA
ON DIPLOMATIC STAGE

For a few short days, some hope remained that the war might be localized, or even stopped altogether. The British tried to persuade the Germans to withdraw; third parties, both official and private, tried to mediate. None of these efforts resulted in any concessions on either side, and on September 3, 1939, Great Britain and France declared war on Germany, thus honoring their treaty obligations to Poland. Paul Schmidt, the German foreign ministry's chief interpreter, describes the final scene in his memoirs.

It was past midnight when the British embassy phoned the Reich Chancellery. Henderson,[1] they said, had just received instructions from London to convey a communication from the British government the next morning at 9:00, and was requesting that Ribbentrop receive him at the foreign ministry at that time. It was clear that this communication would contain nothing pleasant, that it might in fact be a true ultimatum. Ribbentrop, therefore, did not show the least desire to receive the British ambassador in person the next morning. As luck would have it, I happened to be standing near him. "Actually, I think that you could receive the ambassador in

Source: Paul Schmidt, *Statist auf diplomatischer Bühne* (Athenäum-Verlag, Bonn, 1949), pp. 462–464 (translated by the editor).
[1] Sir Nevile Henderson, British ambassador to Berlin.

my place," he said to me. "Why don't you have someone ask the British whether they'd mind. We can tell them that the foreign minister is otherwise engaged." The British did not mind, and I was instructed to receive Henderson the next morning, or, more accurately, in five hours, since meanwhile it was 4:00 a.m.

On Sunday, September 3, 1939, I had, because of the recent days' excitement, woken up so late at home that I reached the foreign ministry only with the aid of a taxicab. As we drove across the Wilhelmsplatz we were just in time to see Henderson entering Wilhelmstrasse 76 through its historic door. I used a side door, and was ready to receive Henderson at precisely nine o'clock in Ribbentrop's study. And it was precisely at nine that the usher announced him. He entered the room with a very serious face, shook my hand, but did not follow my invitation to sit down at the small table in the corner of the room. Instead, he solemnly stood in the middle of the room. "Unfortunately I must, by order of my government, hand you an ultimatum to the German government," he began in an emotional voice, and then read, while we stood facing each other, the familiar document from the British government. "More than twenty-four hours have passed since an immediate answer to the warning of September 1 was requested, and since the attacks on Poland have grown in intensity. If His Majesty's Government does not receive, by eleven o'clock British summer time, satisfactory assurances regarding the cessation of all aggressive actions against Poland, and the withdrawal of German troops from that country, from that time on a state of war shall exist between Great Britain and Germany."

After these words, Henderson gave me the portentous document, and said his good byes. "I am truly sorry," he said, "that it had to be you to whom I am handing this document, for you have always been so helpful." I, for my part, expressed my regrets as well, and found some genuinely fond words of farewell for the British ambassador whom, as I said before, I had always held in high esteem.

Then I went, with the ultimatum in my briefcase, to the Reich Chancellery, where everyone was waiting in great suspense. Most of the cabinet members and high party functionaries were assembled in the room next to Hitler's study. There was quite a crowd, and I had some trouble in making my way through it to Hitler's room. "What's the news," several rather fearful sounding voices asked me.

"School's out today," was all I said, shrugging my shoulders. I entered the next room, where Hitler sat at his desk, while Ribbentrop, somewhat to the right of him, stood by the window. I stopped at some distance from Hitler's table and slowly translated the ultimatum of the British government. When I finished, there was complete silence, just as there had been after the drumbeat of the night of Godesberg.[2]

Hitler sat as though he had turned to stone, and looked directly in front of him. He did not lose his composure, as some people later claimed, nor did he fly into a rage. He just sat there, completely quiet and motionless. After a while, which seemed like an eternity to me, he turned to Ribbentrop, who stood by the window like a man benumbed. "What now?" Hitler asked his foreign minister with a furious glance in his eyes, as though he wished to say that Ribbentrop had misinformed him about the likely reaction of the British. In a soft voice, Ribbentrop replied, "I assume that in the next hour the French will hand us an identical ultimatum."

Since my task was finished, I retired, and told the men waiting in the antechamber who were now crowding around me, "The British have just handed us an ultimatum. Two hours from now, a state of war will exist between England and Germany." Here, too, deadly quiet followed my announcement. Göring turned to me and said, "If we lose this war, may heaven have mercy on us." Goebbels stood in a corner, depressed and alone with his thoughts, and displaying all the charm of a dog caught in the rain. I saw worried faces everywhere, even among the lesser party functionaries in the room.

Shortly afterwards, Coulondre[3] handed Ribbentrop an identical ultimatum with a 5:00 p.m. deadline.

In the evening, I left a blacked-out Berlin in an eastward direction, riding in the foreign ministry's special train. By some irony of fate, the train left from the same loading platform of the Anhalter freight station from which, in a freight train, I had left my home town as a soldier in 1917.

---

[2] The reference is to the conversation between Hitler and Chamberlain at Godesberg on September 23, 1938, which was suddenly interrupted by the news of Czech mobilization. It was, Schmidt recalled, like a drumbeat in a symphony. Following it there was, "for a few beats, complete silence. But then the violins began playing again softly," and the conversation continued, though "in a rather more muted mood than before." (Schmidt, *Statist auf diplomatischer Bühne*, pp. 405–406).

[3] Robert Coulondre, French ambassador to Berlin.

CHAPTER FOUR

World at War: Poland to Pearl Harbor

PRESS DIRECTIVES

Yet any reminiscences of World War I soon seemed irrelevant. For the Germans, under Hitler, were achieving what had eluded them in 1914: the absence of a two-front war, and victory in the West. Threats of *Blitzkrieg* had been no bluff. The war against Poland did proceed with lightning speed. Less than four weeks after the Germans had crossed the border, the last Polish city to hold out, the capital itself, surrendered, and the campaign was over. The Russians, rather than overrunning East Prussia, as they had in World War I, remained neutral—benevolently so. They aided the Germans with supplies, and cooperated in the conquest of Poland by occupying, in mid-September, their half of the country, which had been promised them under the Nazi-Soviet pact. And in the spring and summer of 1940, after the peace offers that Hitler extended to the West had been turned down, it was *Blitzkrieg* once more: quick German victories in the north against Denmark and Norway in April, to provide bases against Britain, and in May, the invasion of Holland and Belgium, followed by the conquest of France in June.

Only Britain now remained in the war, and it was a Britain weakened by the loss of some of its expeditionary force, and of nearly all of that force's supplies, in France. On the other hand, Britain had a great potential ally, the United States. Nominally, the United States was neutral, but from the first, the trend of American legislation, and of American opinion, favored Hitler's enemies. Thus the amended Neutrality Act of 1939, while still prohibiting American loans to the nations at war, and making it unlawful for American ships to transport military supplies to the war zone, did permit belligerents to purchase, and remove, munitions and other supplies at their own risk. This was the famous "cash and carry" system. It was a system that clearly favored the Allies, since the Germans had neither the dollars nor the safe shipping to avail themselves of its provisions.

Yet the Germans would not let themselves be provoked. From the very first, they had a fairly shrewd idea of the direction in which America was moving. Still, the Nazi press, even before the debate over cash and carry had run its course, was told to be circumspect in its treatment of the United States. It was an instruction that, with only minor modifications, was to hold for the next two years.

. . . Extreme restraint is to be used in dealing with all problems concerning the *United States.* Of course Roosevelt is not being honest when he says that the country's neutrality legislation is now in force. He tries, in this fashion, to play the man of peace, since he knows that for the moment, the American public is not ready for

Source: Zeitschriften-Dienst, No. 8o6 (September 23, 1939), p. 2 (translated by the editor).

measures which would make the entry of the United States into the conflict an immediate prospect. What he wants to do is to gain time. In the meanwhile, he uses his entire propaganda machine to influence the American public in an anti-German direction. On the other hand, the good sense of the American public is not to be underestimated; the isolationists are not without support. Whether, and for how long, they will succeed in resisting the joint assault of Rooseveltian, Jewish, and British propaganda is something that cannot be predicted yet. Our guideline remains: restraint, and no undue emphasis on anti-war voices (so as not to embarrass the speakers). No doubts about the maintenance of U. S. neutrality.

2. FRANKLIN D. ROOSEVELT

THE HAND THAT HELD THE DAGGER

The restraint of Germany's media made little or no impact on the United States. Cash and carry was followed by even more patently unneutral words and acts. Characteristic of the former was the speech that President Roosevelt gave at Charlottesville, Virginia, on June 10, 1940, the day after Italy had joined its Axis partner in the final stages of the war against France. It was not often that the head of a nation spoke in such terms about other nations with which, in name at least, no state of war existed. But America, in truth, was no longer neutral. It had passed, with this speech, from neutrality to nonbelligerency, from trying to prevent a repetition of 1917 to the open support of those who stood in Hitler's way.

President Newcomb, my friends of the University of Virginia:

. . . Every generation of young men and women in America has questions to ask the world. Most of the time they are the simple but nevertheless difficult questions, questions of work to do, opportunities to find, ambitions to satisfy.

Source: *The Public Papers and Addresses of Franklin D. Roosevelt*, Vol. IX (The Macmillan Company, New York, 1941), pp. 259–264.

But every now and again in the history of the Republic a different kind of question presents itself—a question that asks, not about the future of an individual or even of a generation, but about the future of the country, the future of the American people.

There was such a time at the beginning of our history as a Nation. Young people asked themselves in those days what lay ahead, not for themselves, but for the new United States.

There was such a time again in the seemingly endless years of the War Between the States. Young men and young women on both sides of the line asked themselves, not what trades or professions they would enter, what lives they would make, but what was to become of the country they had known.

There is such a time again today. Again today the young men and the young women of America ask themselves with earnestness and with deep concern this same question: "What is to become of the country we know?"

Now they ask it with even greater anxiety than before. They ask, not only what the future holds for this Republic, but what the future holds for all peoples and all nations that have been living under democratic forms of Government—under the free institutions of a free people.

It is understandable to all of us that they should ask this question. They read the words of those who are telling them that the ideal of individual liberty, the ideal of free franchise, the ideal of peace through justice, are decadent ideals. They read the word and hear the boast of those who say that a belief in force—force directed by self-chosen leaders—is the new and vigorous system which will overrun the earth. They have seen the ascendancy of this philosophy of force in nation after nation where free institutions and individual liberties were once maintained.

It is natural and understandable that the younger generation should first ask itself what the extension of the philosophy of force to all the world would lead to ultimately. We see today in stark reality some of the consequences of what we call the machine age.

Where control of machines has been retained in the hands of mankind as a whole, untold benefits have accrued to mankind. For mankind was then the master; and the machine was the servant.

But in this new system of force the mastery of the machine is not in the hands of mankind. It is in the control of infinitely small groups of individuals who rule without a single one of the democratic sanctions that we have known. The machine in hands of irresponsible conquerors becomes the master; mankind is not only the servant; it is the victim, too. Such mastery abandons with deliberate contempt all the moral values to which even this young country for more than three hundred years has been accustomed and dedicated.

Surely the new philosophy proves from month to month that it could have no possible conception of the way of life or the way of thought of a nation whose origins go back to Jamestown and Plymouth Rock.

Conversely, neither those who spring from that ancient stock nor those who have come hither in later years can be indifferent to the destruction of freedom in their ancestral lands across the sea.

Perception of danger to our institutions may come slowly or it may come with a rush and a shock as it has to the people of the United States in the past few months. This perception of danger has come to us clearly and overwhelmingly; and we perceive the peril in a world-wide arena—an arena that may become so narrowed that only the Americas will retain the ancient faiths.

Some indeed still hold to the now somewhat obvious delusion that we of the United States can safely permit the United States to become a lone island, a lone island in a world dominated by the philosophy of force.

Such an island may be the dream of those who still talk and vote as isolationists. Such an island represents to me and to the overwhelming majority of Americans today a helpless nightmare of a people without freedom—the nightmare of a people lodged in prison, handcuffed, hungry, and fed through the bars from day to day by the contemptuous, unpitying masters of other continents.

It is natural also that we should ask ourselves how now we can prevent the building of that prison and the placing of ourselves in the midst of it.

Let us not hesitate—all of us—to proclaim certain truths. Overwhelmingly we, as a nation—and this applies to all the other American nations—are convinced that military and naval victory for the gods of force and hate would endanger the institutions of democracy in the western world, and that equally, therefore, the whole of our sympathies lies with those nations that are giving their life blood in combat against these forces.

The people and the Government of the United States have seen with the utmost regret and with grave disquiet the decision of the Italian Government to engage in the hostilities now raging in Europe.

More than three months ago the Chief of the Italian Government sent me word that because of the determination of Italy to limit, so far as might be possible, the spread of the European conflict, more than two hundred millions of people in the region of the Mediterranean had been enabled to escape the suffering and the devastation of war.

I informed the Chief of the Italian Government that this desire on the part of Italy to prevent the war from spreading met with full sympathy and response on the part of the Government and the people of the United States, and I expressed the earnest hope of this Government and of this people that this policy on the part of Italy might be continued. I made it clear that in the opinion of the Government of the United States any extension of hostilities in the region of the Mediterranean might result in a still greater enlargement of the scene of the conflict, the conflict in the Near East and in Africa and that if this came to pass no one could foretell how much greater the theater of the war eventually might become.

Again on a subsequent occasion, not so long ago, recognizing that certain aspirations of Italy might form the basis of discussions among the powers most specifically concerned, I offered, in a message addressed to the Chief of the Italian Government, to send to the Governments of France and of Great Britain such specific indications of the desires of Italy to obtain readjustments with regard to her position as the Chief of the Italian Government might desire to transmit through me. While making it clear that the Government of the United States in such an event could not and would not assume responsibility for the nature of the proposals submitted nor for agreements which might thereafter be reached, I proposed that if Italy would refrain from entering the war I would be willing to ask assurances from the other powers concerned that they would faithfully execute any agreement so reached and that Italy's voice in any future peace conference would have the same authority as if Italy had actually taken part in the war, as a belligerent.

Unfortunately to the regret of all of us and the regret of humanity, the Chief of the Italian Government was unwilling to accept the procedure suggested and he has made no counter proposal.

This Government directed its efforts to doing what it could to work for the preservation of peace in the Mediterranean area, and it likewise expressed its willingness to endeavor to cooperate with the Government of Italy when the appropriate occasion arose for the creation of a more stable world order, through the reduction of armaments, and through the construction of a more liberal international economic system which would assure to all powers equality of opportunity in the world's markets and in the securing of raw materials on equal terms.

I have likewise, of course, felt it necessary in my communications to Signor Mussolini to express the concern of the Government of the United States because of the fact that any extension of the war in the region of the Mediterranean would inevitably result in great prejudice to the ways of life and Government and to the trade and commerce of all the American Republics.

The Government of Italy has now chosen to preserve what it terms its "freedom of action" and to fulfill what it states are its promises to Germany. In so doing it has manifested disregard for the rights and security of other nations, disregard for the lives of the peoples of those nations which are directly threatened by this spread of the war; and has evidenced its unwillingness to find the means through pacific negotiations for the satisfaction of what it believes are its legitimate aspirations.

On this tenth day of June, 1940, the hand that held the dagger has struck it into the back of its neighbor.

On this tenth day of June, 1940, in this University founded by the first great American teacher of democracy, we send forth our prayers and our hopes to those beyond the seas who are maintaining with magnificent valor their battle for freedom.

In our American unity, we will pursue two obvious and simultaneous courses; we will extend to the opponents of force the material resources of this nation; and, at the same time, we will harness and speed up the use of those resources in order that we ourselves in the Americas may have equipment and training equal to the task of any emergency and every defense.

All roads leading to the accomplishment of these objectives must be kept clear of obstructions. We will not slow down or detour. Signs and signals call for speed—full speed ahead.

It is right that each new generation should ask questions. But in recent months the principal question has been somewhat simplified. Once more the future of the nation and of the American people is at stake.

We need not and we will not, in any way, abandon our continuing effort to make democracy work within our borders. We still insist on the need for vast improvements in our own social and economic life.

But that is a component part of national defense itself.

The program unfolds swiftly and into that program will fit the responsibility and the opportunity of every man and woman in the land to preserve his and her heritage in days of peril.

I call for effort, courage, sacrifice, devotion. Granting the love of freedom, all of these are possible.

And the love of freedom is still fierce and steady in the nation today.

3.   FRANKLIN D. ROOSEVELT

MESSAGE TO
THE CONGRESS

The offer of the "material resources of this nation," which the president had made "to the opponents of force" was more than rhetoric. In response to an urgent British appeal for help, the president, acting on his executive authority, in September 1940 provided Britain with fifty American destroyers in return for the use of eight naval and air bases from Bermuda to British Guiana. In a message to Congress, on September 3, he explained the action he had taken.

I transmit herewith for the information of the Congress notes exchanged between the British Ambassador at Washington and the

Source: Daniel M. Smith, ed., *Major Problems in American Diplomatic History* (D. C. Heath and Company, Boston, 1964), pp. 483–484.

Secretary of State on September 2, 1940,[1] under which this Government has acquired the right to lease naval and air bases in Newfoundland, and in the islands of Bermuda, the Bahamas, Jamaica, St. Lucia, Trinidad, and Antigua, and in British Guiana; also a copy of an opinion of the Attorney General dated August 27, 1940, regarding my authority to consummate this arrangement.

The right to bases in Newfoundland and Bermuda are gifts— generously given and gladly received. The other bases mentioned have been acquired in exchange for fifty of our over-age destroyers.

This is not inconsistent in any sense with our status of peace. Still less is it a threat against any nation. It is an epochal and far-reaching act of preparation for continental defense in the face of grave danger.

Preparation for defense is an inalienable prerogative of a sovereign state. Under present circumstances this exercise of sovereign right is essential to the maintenance of our peace and safety. This is the most important action in the reinforcement of our national defense that has been taken since the Louisiana Purchase. Then as now, considerations of safety from overseas attack were fundamental.

The value to the Western Hemisphere of these outposts of security is beyond calculation. Their need has long been recognized by our country, and especially by those primarily charged with the duty of charting and organizing our own naval and military defense. They are essential to the protection of the Panama Canal, Central America, the Northern portion of South America, The Antilles, Canada, Mexico, and our own Eastern and Gulf Seaboards. Their consequent importance in hemispheric defense is obvious. For these reasons I have taken advantage of the present opportunity to acquire them.

[1] Not printed here. For this exchange, see *U.S. Department of State Bulletin*, September 7, 1940, pp. 199–200.

"FOUR FREEDOMS"*

Four months later, the president, in his annual message to Congress, prepared the way for even broader support to "those resolute peoples, everywhere, who are resisting aggression." It was a speech that combined propaganda—the four freedoms were meant to be in the current war what Wilson's fourteen points had been in the previous one—with a call to action. The United States, as he had suggested in an earlier fireside chat, was to become "the arsenal of democracy."

Mr. President, Mr. Speaker, Members of the Seventy-seventh Congress:

I address you, the Members of the Seventy-seventh Congress, at a moment unprecedented in the history of the Union. I use the word "unprecedented," because at no previous time has American security been as seriously threatened from without as it is today. . . .

Every realist knows that the democratic way of life is at this moment being directly assailed in every part of the world—assailed either by arms, or by secret spreading of poisonous propaganda by those who seek to destroy unity and promote discord in nations that are still at peace.

During sixteen long months this assault has blotted out the whole pattern of democratic life in an appalling number of independent nations, great and small. The assailants are still on the march, threatening other nations, great and small.

Therefore, as your President, performing my constitutional duty to "give to the Congress information of the state of the Union," I find it, unhappily, necessary to report that the future and the safety of our country and of our democracy are overwhelmingly involved in events far beyond our borders.

Armed defense of democratic existence is now being gallantly waged in four continents. If that defense fails, all the population and all the resources of Europe, Asia, Africa and Australasia will be dominated by the conquerors. Let us remember that the total of those populations and their resources in those four continents greatly exceeds the sum total of the population and the resources of the whole of the Western Hemisphere—many times over. . . .

Source: *The Public Papers and Addresses of Franklin D. Roosevelt*, Vol. IX, pp. 663–672.
* Message to the Congress, January 6, 1941.

Our national policy is this:

First, by an impressive expression of the public will and without regard to partisanship, we are committed to all-inclusive national defense.

Second, by an impressive expression of the public will and without regard to partisanship, we are committed to full support of all those resolute peoples, everywhere, who are resisting aggression and are thereby keeping war away from our Hemisphere. By this support, we express our determination that the democratic cause shall prevail; and we strengthen the defense and the security of our own nation.

Third, by an impressive expression of the public will and without regard to partisanship, we are committed to the proposition that principles of morality and considerations for our own security will never permit us to acquiesce in a peace dictated by aggressors and sponsored by appeasers. We know that enduring peace cannot be bought at the cost of other people's freedom.

In the recent national election there was no substantial difference between the two great parties in respect to that national policy. No issue was fought out on this line before the American electorate. Today it is abundantly evident that American citizens everywhere are demanding and supporting speedy and complete action in recognition of obvious danger.

Therefore, the immediate need is a swift and driving increase in our armament production. . . .

New circumstances are constantly begetting new needs for our safety. I shall ask this Congress for greatly increased new appropriations and authorizations to carry on what we have begun.

I also ask this Congress for authority and for funds sufficient to manufacture additional munitions and war supplies of many kinds, to be turned over to those nations which are now in actual war with aggressor nations.

Our most useful and immediate role is to act as an arsenal for them as well as for ourselves. They do not need man power, but they do need billions of dollars worth of the weapons of defense.

The time is near when they will not be able to pay for them all in ready cash. We cannot, and we will not, tell them that they must surrender, merely because of present inability to pay for the weapons which we know they must have.

I do not recommend that we make them a loan of dollars with which to pay for these weapons—a loan to be repaid in dollars.

I recommend that we make it possible for those nations to continue to obtain war materials in the United States, fitting their orders into our own program. Nearly all their matériel would, if the time ever came, be useful for our own defense.

Taking counsel of expert military and naval authorities, considering what is best for our own security, we are free to decide how much should be kept here and how much should be sent abroad to our friends who by their determined and heroic resistance are giving us time in which to make ready our own defense.

For what we send abroad, we shall be repaid within a reasonable time following the close of hostilities, in similar materials, or, at our option, in other goods of many kinds, which they can produce and which we need.

Let us say to the democracies: "We Americans are vitally concerned in your defense of freedom. We are putting forth our energies, our resources and our organizing powers to give you the strength to regain and maintain a free world. We shall send you, in ever-increasing numbers, ships, planes, tanks, guns. This is our purpose and our pledge."

In fulfillment of this purpose we will not be intimidated by the threats of dictators that they will regard as a breach of international law or as an act of war our aid to the democracies which dare to resist their aggression. Such aid is not an act of war, even if a dictator should unilaterally proclaim it so to be.

When the dictators, if the dictators, are ready to make war upon us, they will not wait for an act of war on our part. They did not wait for Norway or Belgium or the Netherlands to commit an act of war.

Their only interest is in a new one-way international law, which lacks mutuality in its observance, and, therefore, becomes an instrument of oppression.

The happiness of future generations of Americans may well depend upon how effective and how immediate we can make our aid felt. . . .

As men do not live by bread alone, they do not fight by armaments alone. Those who man our defenses, and those behind them who build our defenses, must have the stamina and the courage which come from unshakable belief in the manner of life which they are defending. . . .

In the future days, which we seek to make secure, we look forward to a world founded upon four essential human freedoms.

The first is freedom of speech and expression—everywhere in the world.

The second, is freedom of every person to worship God in his own way—everywhere in the world.

The third is freedom from want—which, translated into world terms, means economic understandings which will secure to every nation a healthy peacetime life for its inhabitants—everywhere in the world.

The fourth is freedom from fear—which, translated into world terms, means a world-wide reduction of armaments to such a point and in such a thorough fashion that no nation will be in a position to commit an act of physical aggression against any neighbor—anywhere in the world.

That is no vision of a distant millennium. It is a definite basis for a kind of world attainable in our own time and generation. That kind of world is the very antithesis of the so-called new order of tyranny which the dictators seek to create with the crash of a bomb.

To that new order we oppose the greater conception—the moral order. A good society is able to face schemes of world domination and foreign revolutions alike without fear.

Since the beginning of our American history, we have been engaged in change—in a perpetual peaceful revolution—a revolution which goes on steadily, quietly adjusting itself to changing conditions—without the concentration camp or the quick-lime in the ditch. The world order which we seek is the cooperation of free countries, working together in a friendly, civilized society.

This nation has placed its destiny in the hands and heads and hearts of its millions of free men and women; and its faith in freedom under the guidance of God. Freedom means the supremacy of human rights everywhere. Our support goes to those who struggle to gain those rights or keep them. Our strength is our unity of purpose.

To that high concept there can be no end save victory.

5.

THE LEND-LEASE ACT
OF MARCH 11, 1941

The action suggested in the Four Freedoms speech took concrete form two months later in the Lend-Lease Act. It was a clear departure from earlier neutrality legislation, and in effect let the British prosecute the war with American weapons and American equipment. Not all Americans approved of it, and an often sharp debate ensued in Congress. But in the end, both houses passed the legislation with substantial majorities.

Be it enacted That this Act may be cited as "An Act to Promote the Defense of the United States." . . .

Section 3.

(a) Notwithstanding the provisions of any other law, the President may, from time to time, when he deems it in the interest of national defense, authorize the Secretary of War, the Secretary of the Navy, or the head of any other department or agency of the Government—

(1) To manufacture in arsenals, factories, and shipyards under their jurisdiction, or otherwise procure, to the extent to which funds are made available therefor, or contracts are authorized from time to time by the Congress, or both, any defense article for the government of any country whose defense the President deems vital to the defense of the United States.

(2) To sell, transfer title to, exchange, lease, lend, or otherwise dispose of, to any such government any defense article, but no defense article not manufactured or procured under paragraph (1) shall in any way be disposed of under this paragraph, except after consultation with the Chief of Staff of the Army or the Chief of Naval Operations of the Navy, or both. The value of defense articles disposed of in any way under authority of this paragraph, and procured from funds heretofore appropriated, shall not exceed $1,300,000,000. The value of such defense articles shall be determined by the head of the department or agency concerned or such other department, agency or officer as shall be designated in the

Source: Henry Steele Commager, ed., *Documents of American History*, Ninth Edition, Vol. 2 (Prentice-Hall, Englewood Cliffs, 1973), pp. 449–450.

manner provided in the rules and regulations issued hereunder. Defense articles procured from funds hereafter appropriated to any department or agency of the Government, other than from funds authorized to be appropriated under this Act, shall not be disposed of in any way under authority of this paragraph except to the extent hereafter authorized by the Congress in the Acts appropriating such funds or otherwise.

(3) To test, inspect, prove, repair, outfit, recondition, or otherwise to place in good working order, to the extent to which funds are made available therefore, or contracts are authorized from time to time by the Congress, or both, any defense article for any such government, or to procure any or all such services by private contract.

(4) To communicate to any such government any defense information, pertaining to any defense article furnished to such government under paragraph (2) of this subsection.

(5) To release for export any defense article disposed of in any way under this subsection to any such government.

(b) The terms and conditions upon which any such foreign government receives any aid authorized under subsection (a) shall be those which the President deems satisfactory, and the benefit to the United States may be payment or repayment in kind or property, or any other direct or indirect benefit which the President deems satisfactory.

(c) After June 30, 1943, or after the passage of a concurrent resolution by the two Houses before June 30, 1943, which declares that the powers conferred by or pursuant to subsection (a) are no longer necessary to promote the defense of the United States, neither the President nor the head of any department or agency shall exercise any of the powers conferred by or pursuant to subsection (a); except that until July 1, 1946, any of such powers may be exercised to the extent necessary to carry out a contract or agreement with such a foreign government made before July 1, 1943, or before the passage of such concurrent resolution, whichever is the earlier.

(d) Nothing in this Act shall be construed to authorize or to permit the authorization of convoying vessels by naval vessels of the United States.

(e) Nothing in this Act shall be construed to authorize or to permit the authorization of the entry of any American vessel into a combat area in violation of section 3 of the Neutrality Act of 1939. . . .

Section 8

The Secretaries of War and of the Navy are hereby authorized to purchase or otherwise acquire arms, ammunition, and implements of war produced within the jurisdiction of any country to which section 3 is applicable, whenever the President deems such purchase or acquisition to be necessary in the interests of the defense of the United States.

Section 9

The President may, from time to time, promulgate such rules and regulations as may be necessary and proper to carry out any of the provisions of this Act; and he may exercise any power or authority conferred on him by this Act through such department, agency, or officer as he shall direct.

6.

MEMORANDUM OF THE CONVERSATION BETWEEN THE FÜHRER AND THE CHAIRMAN OF THE COUNCIL OF PEOPLE'S COMMISSARS AND PEOPLE'S COMMISSAR FOR FOREIGN AFFAIRS

There could be little doubt how the president would use the powers delegated to him. Yet German restraint still held; in the voluminous files of the German foreign ministry, one looks in vain for any indication of a protest made from Berlin.

Source: Sontag and Beddie, eds., *Nazi-Soviet Relations*, pp. 226–234.

No need exists, of course, to credit Hitler with too much statesmanship. One reason for his passivity simply was that he had no long-range American policy, except to hope that if he won the war in Europe quickly and decisively enough, the American problem would resolve itself. Another reason was that by this time, he was very much preoccupied with another problem, that of Russia.

Hitler had never been happy over his alliance with Stalin. From the first, the Nazi-Soviet Pact had been a means to an end—the destruction of Poland—rather than a new policy departure. And the Russians seemed to be confirming all his prejudices against them. They tended to be ungenerous allies, insisting that every promise made or implied in the pact be carried out to the last. What was more, they were apparently obstructing his ambitions in southeastern Europe, pursuing aims of their own that did not fit his schemes for a new order.

Still, he tried to save the alliance. During a visit which Molotov (now Soviet premier as well as foreign minister) paid to Berlin in 1940, Hitler held out visions of a new Tilsit to his Russian visitor. Just as Napoleon and Tsar Alexander once had, so Germany and Russia would now divide the world between them. Molotov responded to these utopian offers with profound prose, and some bothersome questions of detail. Just what were Germany's intentions in Finland? Precisely what were to be Russia's rights in Bulgaria?

Implicit in these questions was that Russia preferred immediate, and concrete, advantages to future prospects of world empire. Implicit, too, was that the Russians did not quite share Hitler's basic assumption that the war was all but won, that just as soon as the weather seemed right, the Führer would strike "the great and final blow against England." (It was a point that Paul Schmidt, a man with a sense of humor, who recorded the meeting, also could not restrain himself from making, as may be seen in the final paragraph of the memorandum.)

STATE SECRET   BERLIN, November 16, 1940

After some words of welcome, the Führer stated that the idea that was uppermost in his mind in the conversations now taking place was this: In the life of peoples it was indeed difficult to lay down a course for development over a long period in the future and the outbreak of conflicts was often strongly influenced by personal factors; he believed, nevertheless, that an attempt had to be made to fix the development of nations, even for a long period of time, in so far as that was possible, so that friction would be avoided and the elements of conflict precluded as far as humanly possible. This was particularly in order when two nations such as the German and Russian nations had at their helm men who possessed sufficient authority to commit their countries to a development in a definite direction. In the case of Russia and Germany, moreover, two very great nations were involved which need not by nature have any conflict of interests, if each nation understood that the other required certain vital necessities without the guarantee of which its existence was impossible. Besides this, both countries had systems of government which did not wage war for the sake of war, but which needed peace more than war in order to carry out their domestic tasks. With due regard for vital needs, particularly in the economic field, it should really be possible to achieve a settlement between them, which would lead to peaceful collaboration between the two countries beyond the life span of the present leaders.

After Molotov had expressed his entire agreement with these arguments, the Führer continued that it was obviously a difficult task to chart developments between peoples and countries over a long period. He believed, however, that it would be possible to elaborate clearly and precisely certain general points of view quite independently of personal motives and to orient the political and economic interests of peoples in such a manner as to give some guarantee that conflicts would be avoided even for rather long periods. The situation in which the conversation of today was taking place was characterized by the fact that Germany was at war, while Soviet Russia was not. Many of the measures taken by Germany had been influenced by the fact of her belligerency. Many of the steps that were necessary in the course of the war had developed from the conduct of the war itself and could not have been anticipated at the outbreak of war. By and large, not only Germany but also Russia had gained great advantages. On further consideration, the political collaboration during the one year of its existence had been of considerable value to both countries.

Molotov stated that this was quite correct.

The Führer declared further that probably neither of the two peoples had realized its wishes 100 percent. In political life, however, even a 20–25 percent realization of demands was worth a good deal. He believed that not every wish would be fulfilled in the future either, but that the two greatest peoples of Europe, if they went along together, would, in any case, gain more than if they worked against each other. If they stood together, some advantage would always accrue to both countries. If they worked against each other, however, third countries would be the sole gainers.

Molotov replied that the argument of the Führer was entirely correct and would be confirmed by history; that it was particularly applicable to the present situation, however.

The Führer then went on to say that proceeding from these ideas he had again quite soberly pondered the question of German-Russian collaboration, at a time when the military operations were in effect concluded.

The war had, moreover, led to complications which were not intended by Germany, but which had compelled her from time to time to react militarily to certain events. The Führer then outlined to Molotov the course of military operations up to the present, which had led to the fact that England no longer had an ally on the continent. He described in detail the military operations now being carried out against England, and he stressed the influence of atmospheric conditions on these operations. The English retaliatory measures were ridiculous, and the Russian gentleman could convince themselves at first hand of the fiction of alleged destruction in Berlin. As soon as atmospheric conditions improved, Germany would be poised for the great and final blow against England. At the moment, then, it was her aim to try not only to make military preparations for this final struggle, but also to clarify the political issues which would be of importance during and after this showdown. He had, therefore, reexamined the relations with Russia, and not in a negative spirit, but with the intention of organizing them positively—if possible, for a long period of time. In so doing he had reached several conclusions:

1. Germany was not seeking to obtain military aid from Russia;

2. Because of the tremendous extension of the war, Germany had been forced, in order to oppose England, to penetrate into territories remote from her and in which she was not basically interested politically or economically;

3. There were nevertheless certain requirements, the full importance of which had become apparent only during the war, but which were absolutely vital to Germany. Among them were certain sources of raw materials which were considered by Germany as most vital and absolutely indispensable. Possibly Herr Molotov was of the opinion that in one case or another they had departed from the conception of the spheres of influence which had been agreed upon by Stalin and the Reich Foreign Minister. Such departures had already occurred in some cases in the course of Russian operations against Poland. In a number of cases, on calm considera-

tion of the German and Russian interests, he (the Führer) had not been ready to make concessions, but he had realized that it was desirable to meet the needs of Russia half-way, as, for instance, in the case of Lithuania. From an economic point of view, Lithuania had, it is true, had a certain importance for us, but from a political point of view, we had understood the necessity of straightening out the situation in this whole field in order thereby to prevent in the future the spiritual revival of tendencies that were capable of causing tension between the two countries of Germany and Russia. In another case, namely, that of the South Tyrol, Germany had taken a similar position. However, in the course of the war, factors had arisen for Germany which could not have been anticipated at the outbreak of the war, but which had to be considered absolutely vital from the standpoint of military operations.

He (the Führer) now had pondered the question how, beyond all petty momentary considerations, further to clarify in bold outline the collaboration between Germany and Russia and what direction future German-Russian developments should take. In this matter the following viewpoints were of importance for Germany:

1. Need for *Lebensraum* [*Raumnot*]. During the war Germany had acquired such large areas that she would require one hundred years to utilize them fully.

2. Some colonial expansion in Central Africa was necessary.

3. Germany needed certain raw materials, the supply of which she would have to safeguard under all circumstances. And

4. She could not permit the establishment by hostile powers of air or naval bases in certain areas.

In no event, however, would the interests of Russia be affected. The Russian empire could develop without in the least prejudicing German interests. (Molotov said this was quite correct.) If both countries came to realize this fact, they could collaborate to their mutual advantage and could spare themselves difficulties, friction, and nervous tension. It was perfectly obvious that Germany and Russia would never become one world. Both countries would always exist separate from each other as two powerful elements of the world. Each of them could shape its future as it liked, if in so doing it considered the interest of the other. Germany herself had no interests in Asia other than general economic and commercial interest. In particular, she had no colonial interests there. She knew, furthermore, that the possible colonial territories in Asia would probably fall to Japan. If by any chance China, too, should be drawn into the orbit of the awakening nations, any colonial aspirations would be doomed to disappointment from the start in view of the masses of people living there.

There were in Europe a number of points of contact between Germany, Russia, and Italy. Each one of these three countries had an understandable desire for an outlet to the open sea. Germany wanted to get out of the North Sea, Italy wanted to remove the barrier of Gibraltar, and Russia was also striving toward the ocean. The question now was how much chance there was for these great countries really to obtain free access to the ocean without in turn coming into conflict with each other over the matter. This was also the viewpoint from which he looked upon the organization of European relations after the war. The leading statesmen of Europe must prevent this war from becoming the father of a new war. The issues to be settled had, therefore, to be settled in such a manner that, at least in the foreseeable future, no new conflict could arise.

In this spirit, he (the Führer) had talked with the French statesmen and believed that he had found among them some sympathy for a settlement which would lead to tolerable conditions for a rather long period and which would be of advantage to all concerned, if only to the extent that a new war did not again have to be feared immediately. Referring to the preamble of the Armistice Treaty with France, he had pointed out to Pétain and Laval that, as long as the war with England lasted, no step might be taken which would in any way be incompatible with the conditions for ending this war against Great Britain.

Elsewhere, too, there were problems such as these, but ones which arose only for the duration of the war. Thus, for instance, Germany had no political interests whatsoever in the Balkans and was active there at present exclusively under the compulsion of securing for herself certain raw materials. It was a matter of purely military interests, the safeguarding of which was not a pleasant task, since, for instance, as German military force had to be maintained in Rumania, hundreds of kilometers away from the supply centers.

For similar reasons the idea was intolerable to Germany that England might get a foothold in Greece in order to establish air and naval bases there. The Reich was compelled to prevent this under any circumstances.

The continuation of the war under such circumstances was of

course not desirable. And that is why Germany had wanted to end the war after the conclusion of the Polish campaign. At that time England and France could have had peace without personal sacrifices; they had, however, preferred to continue the war. Of course, blood also creates rights, and it was inadmissible that certain countries should have declared and waged war without afterward paying the cost. He (the Führer) had made this clear to the French. At the present stage of developments, however, the question was which of the countries responsible for the war had to pay more. At any rate, Germany would have preferred to end the war last year and to have demobilized her army in order to resume her peacetime work, since from an economic point of view any war was bad business. Even the victor had to incur such expenses before, during, and after the war that he could have reached his goal much more cheaply in a peaceful development.

Molotov concurred in this idea, stating that in any case it was vastly more expensive to attain a goal by military measures than by peaceful means. The Führer pointed out further that under the present circumstances Germany had been forced by wartime developments to become active in areas in which she was politically disinterested but had at most economic interests. Self-preservation, however, absolutely dictated this course. Nevertheless, this activity of Germany—forced upon her in the areas in question—represented no obstacle to any pacification of the world which would later be undertaken, and which would bring to the nations working toward the same end that for which they hoped.

In addition, there was the problem of America. The United States was now pursuing an imperialistic policy. It was not fighting for England, but only trying to get the British Empire into its grasp. They were helping England, at best, in order to further their own rearmament and to reinforce their military power by acquiring bases. In the distant future it would be a question of establishing a great solidarity among those countries which might be involved in case of an extension of the sphere of influence of this Anglo-Saxon power, which had a more solid foundation, by far, than England. In this case, it was not a question of the immediate future; not in 1945, but in 1970 or 1980, at the earliest, would the freedom of other nations be seriously endangered by this Anglo-Saxon power. At any rate, the Continent of Europe had to adjust itself now to this development and had to act jointly against the Anglo-Saxons and against any of their attempts to acquire dangerous bases. Therefore, he had undertaken an exchange of ideas with France, Italy, and Spain, in order with these countries to set up in the whole of Europe and Africa some kind of Monroe Doctrine and to adopt a new joint colonial policy by which each of the powers concerned would claim for itself only as much colonial territory as it could really utilize. In other regions, where Russia was the power in the foremost position, the interests of the latter would, of course, have to come first. This would result in a great coalition of powers which, guided by sober appraisal of realities, would have to establish their respective spheres of interest and would assert themselves against the rest of the world correspondingly. It was surely a difficult task to organize such a coalition of countries; and yet, to conceive it was not as difficult as to carry it out.

The Führer then reverted to the German-Russian efforts. He understood thoroughly Russia's attempts to get ice-free ports with absolutely secure access to the open sea. Germany had enormously expanded her *Lebensraum* in her present eastern provinces. At least half of this area, however, must be regarded as an economic liability. Probably both Russia and Germany had not achieved everything they had set out to do. In any case, however, the successes had been great on both sides. If a liberal view were taken of the remaining issues and due regard were taken of the fact that Germany was still at war and had to concern herself with areas which, in and for themselves, were of no importance to her politically, substantial gains for both partners could be achieved in the future, too. In this connection the Führer again turned to the Balkans and repeated that Germany would at once oppose by military action any attempt by England to get a foothold in Salonika. She still retained unpleasant memories from the last war of the then Salonika Front.

To a question of Molotov's as to how Salonika constituted a danger, the Führer referred to the proximity of the Rumanian petroleum fields, which Germany wished to protect under all circumstances. As soon as peace prevailed, however, the German troops would immediately leave Rumania again.

In the further course of the conversation, the Führer asked Molotov how Russia planned to safeguard her interests in the Black Sea and in the Straits. Germany would also be prepared at any time to help effect an improvement for Russia in the régime of the Straits.

Molotov replied that the statements of the Führer had been of a general nature and that in general he could agree with his reasoning. He was also of the opinion that it would be in the interest of Germany and the Soviet Union if the two countries would collaborate and not fight each other. Upon his departure from Moscow, Stalin had given him exact instructions, and everything that he was about to say was identical with the views of Stalin. He concurred in the opinion of the Führer that both partners had derived substantial benefits from the German-Russian agreement. Germany had received a secure hinterland that, as was generally known, had been of great importance for the further course of events during the year of war. In Poland, too, Germany had gained considerable economic advantages. By the exchange of Lithuania for the Voivodeship of Lublin, all possible friction between Russia and Germany had been avoided. The German-Russian agreement of last year could therefore be regarded as fulfilled, except for one point, namely, Finland. The Finnish question was still unsolved, and he asked the Führer to tell him whether the German-Russian agreement, as far as it concerned Finland, was still in force. In the opinion of the Soviet Government, no changes had occurred here. Also, in the opinion of the Soviet Government, the German-Russian agreement of last year represented only a partial solution. In the meanwhile, other issues had arisen that also had to be solved.

Molotov then turned to the matter of the significance of the Tripartite Pact. What was the meaning of the New Order in Europe and in Asia, and what role would the U.S.S.R. be given in it? These issues must be discussed during the Berlin conversations and during the contemplated visit of the Reich Foreign Minister to Moscow, on which the Russians were definitely counting. Morever, there were issues to be clarified regarding Russia's Balkan and Black Sea interests with respect to Bulgaria, Rumania, and Turkey. It would be easier for the Russian Government to give specific replies to the questions raised by the Führer, if it could obtain the explanations just requested. It would be interested in the New Order in Europe, and particularly in the tempo and the form of this New Order. It would also like to have an idea of the boundaries of the so-called Greater East Asian Sphere.

The Führer replied that the Tripartite Pact was intended to regulate conditions in Europe as to the natural interests of the European countries and, consequently, Germany was now approaching the Soviet Union in order that she might express herself regarding the areas of interest to her. In no case was a settlement to be made without Soviet Russian cooperation. This applied not only to Europe, but also to Asia, where Russia herself was to cooperate in the definition of the Greater East Asian Sphere and where she was to designate her claims there. Germany's task in this case was that of a mediator. Russia by no means was to be confronted with a *fait accompli.*

When the Führer undertook to try to establish the above-mentioned coalition of powers, it was not the German-Russian relationship which appeared to him to be the most difficult point, but the question of whether a collaboration between Germany, France, and Italy was possible. Only now that he believed this problem could be solved, and after a settlement in broad outlines had in effect been accepted by the three countries, had he thought it possible to contact Soviet Russia for the purpose of settling the questions of the Black Sea, the Balkans, and Turkey.

In conclusion, the Führer summed up by stating that the discussion, to a certain extent, represented the first concrete step toward a comprehensive collaboration, with due consideration for the problems of Western Europe, which were to be settled between Germany, Italy, and France, as well as for the issues of the East, which were essentially the concern of Russia and Japan, but in which Germany offered her good offices as mediator. It was a matter of opposing any attempt on the part of America to "make money on Europe." The United States had no business either in Europe, in Africa, or in Asia.

Molotov expressed his agreement with the statements of the Führer regarding the role of America and England. The participation of Russia in the Tripartite Pact appeared to him entirely acceptable in principle, provided that Russia was to cooperate as a partner and not be merely an object. In that case he saw no difficulties in the matter of participation of the Soviet Union in the common effort. But the aim and the significance of the Pact must first be more closely defined, particularly because of the delimitation of the Greater East Asian Sphere.

In view of a possible air raid alarm the talk was broken off at this point and postponed until the following day, the Führer promising Molotov that he would discuss with him in detail the various issues which had come up during the conversation.

SCHMIDT

7. COUNT WERNER VON DER SCHULENBURG*

TO THE GERMAN FOREIGN MINISTRY

The questions were discussed not just the next day, but in the follow-up negotiations in Moscow as well. At the end of November, the Russian reply was ready. Its demands were even more specific, and far-reaching, than those made by Molotov in Berlin. Communist Russia's ambitions, it appeared, could be quite as grand as Nazi Germany's.

Telegram

VERY URGENT   Moscow, November 26, 1940—5:34 a.m.
STRICTLY SECRET   Received November 26, 1940—8:50 a.m.
No. 2362 of November 25

For the Reich Minister in person.

Molotov asked me to call on him this evening and . . . stated the following:

The Soviet Government has studied the contents of the statements of the Reich Foreign Minister in the concluding conversation on November 13 and takes the following stand:

"The Soviet Government is prepared to accept the draft of the Four Power Pact which the Reich Foreign Minister outlined in the

Source: Sontag and Beddie, eds., *Nazi-Soviet Relations*, pp. 258–259.
* German ambassador to the Soviet Union.

conversation of November 13, regarding political collaboration and reciprocal economic support subject to the following conditions:

"1) Provided that the German troops are immediately withdrawn from Finland, which, under the compact of 1939, belongs to the Soviet Union's sphere of influence. At the same time the Soviet Union undertakes to ensure peaceful relations with Finland and to protect German economic interests in Finland (export of lumber and nickel).

"2) Provided that within the next few months the security of the Soviet Union in the Straits is assured by the conclusion of a mutual assistance pact between the Soviet Union and Bulgaria, which geographically is situated inside the security zone of the Black Sea boundaries of the Soviet Union, and by the establishment of a base for land and naval forces of the U.S.S.R. within range of the Bosporus and the Dardanelles by means of a long-term lease.

"3) Provided that the area south of Batum and Baku in the general direction of the Persian Gulf is recognized as the center of the aspirations of the Soviet Union.

"4) Provided that Japan renounces her rights to concessions for coal and oil in Northern Sakhalin.

"In accordance with the foregoing, the draft of the protocol concerning the delimitation of the spheres of influence as outlined by the Reich Foreign Minister would have to be amended so as to stipulate the focal point of the aspirations of the Soviet Union south of Batum and Baku in the general direction of the Persian Gulf.

"Likewise, the draft of the protocol or agreement between Germany, Italy, and the Soviet Union with respect to Turkey should be amended so as to guarantee a base for light naval and land forces of the U.S.S.R. on the Bosporus and the Dardanelles by means of a long-term lease, including—in case Turkey declares herself willing to join the Four Power Pact—a guarantee of the independence and of the territory of Turkey by the three countries named.

"This protocol should provide that in case Turkey refuses to join the Four Powers, Germany, Italy, and the Soviet Union agree to work out and to carry through the required military and diplomatic measures, and a separate agreement to this effect should be concluded.

"Furthermore there should be agreement upon:

- "*a*) a third secret protocol between Germany and the Soviet Union concerning Finland (see Point 1 above).

- "*b*) a fourth secret protocol between Japan and the Soviet Union concerning the renunciation by Japan of the oil and coal concession in Northern Sakhalin (in return for an adequate compensation).

- "*c*) a fifth secret protocol between Germany, the Soviet Union, and Italy, recognizing that Bulgaria is geographically located inside the security zone of the Black Sea boundaries of the Soviet Union and that it is therefore a political necessity that a mutual assistance pact be concluded between the Soviet Union and Bulgaria, which in no way shall affect the internal regime of Bulgaria, her sovereignty or independence."

In conclusion Molotov stated that the Soviet proposal provided for five protocols instead of the two envisaged by the Reich Foreign Minister. He would appreciate a statement of the German view.

SCHULENBURG

8.   ADOLF HITLER

FÜHRER DIRECTIVE NO. 21

Hitler's response came in the form of an instruction to the German armed forces. He had tried to work with the Russians and failed; it was back to *Mein Kampf* now.

TOP SECRET   FÜHRER'S HEADQUARTERS,
BY OFFICER ONLY   December 18, 1940

DIRECTIVE NO. 21
OPERATION BARBAROSSA

The German Armed Forces must be prepared *to crush Soviet Russia in a quick campaign* (Operation Barbarossa) even before the conclusion of the war against England.

Source: Sontag and Beddie, eds., *Nazi-Soviet Relations*, p. 260.

For this purpose the *Army* will have to employ all available units, with the reservation that the occupied territories must be secured against surprise attacks.

For the *Air Force* it will be a matter of releasing such strong forces for the eastern campaign in support of the Army that a quick completion of the ground operations may be expected and that damage to Eastern German territory by enemy air attacks will be as slight as possible. . . .

9.

HEINRICH HIMMLER

"ONCE MORE, THE GOTHS ARE RIDING"

On June 22, 1941, along a 2,000 mile front, the attack began. Operation Barbarossa had become bloody earnest. That this was no ordinary war, no old-fashioned conflict of interest that conventional diplomacy had failed to resolve, was clear to anyone who cared to read *Mein Kampf*. And for those who did not, German propaganda supplied some obvious reminders. Here was the way the leader of the SS put it to his men. (Privately, a year later, he said it even more bluntly. "The social question," he said after a visit to occupied Russia, "can only be solved by killing the others off, so we get their land.")

. . . That which the Goths, the Varangians, and all the individual migrants of Germanic blood failed to achieve, that we now shall—a new Teutonic migration, brought about by our Leader, the Leader of all Teutons. Now we shall beat back the storm of the steppe, now we shall finally secure Europe's eastern border. Now there will be fulfilled what Germanic fighters once dreamt of in the forests and vastnesses of the East. A 3000-year-old chapter of history today reaches its glorious conclusion. Once again, since June 1941, the Goths are riding—each one of us a Teutonic fighter! . . .

Source: SS Leitheft, VII, No. 9b, in Walter Hofer, ed., *Der Nationalsozialismus* (Fischer Bücherei, Frankfurt, 1958), p. 250 (translated by the editor).

AN EDITORIAL

After the invasion of Russia, a few American isolationists were more determined than ever to keep the country out of war. Morally and ideologically, Soviet Communism seemed as repugnant as German Nazism; perhaps the world might be lucky enough to see the two systems kill each other off. But a majority of Americans realized that the country was even closer to a shooting war now than it had been before. An editorial in the *Saturday Evening Post*, the first to appear after the attack on Russia, was symptomatic of this attitude. The *Post* had opposed America's involvement, and still did. It had inveighed against the massive foreign propaganda effort aimed at America, and still did. It had wished a plague on both Hitler's and Stalin's houses, and still did. But there was an air of resignation now. No "intelligent doubt" seemed left about where Roosevelt's policies were taking the nation.

THE FOREIGN MALADY

One effect of Hitler's murderous assault upon his Russian partner in aggressor crime was to make vivid in this country certain extreme and ugly symptoms of the foreign malady. We think no American could ponder what was thereby revealed without a sense of foreboding and sickness of heart.

The news broke on Saturday night, after the Sunday newspapers had gone to press, and for many homes radio was the only means of dissemination.

Two thoughts were immediately present.

The first was to ask whether the Soviet government with its hands still foul from the rape of Finland on its own account and the cynical murder of Poland in joint account with Hitler, would now be received among the defenders of freedom and have access to the arsenal of democracy.

The second was satirical. Now the sabotage strikes in American defense industries would cease, by a new Communist Party line.

The question that came first was answered Sunday afternoon, not by the American Government but by the British government. Winston Churchill came on the radio, saying any hand against

Source: The Saturday Evening Post, August 2, 1941, p. 26.

Hitler was welcome, even the hand of Stalin, although, as he himself had often said and would not unsay, this was the hideous hand of a slayer of freedom. "It follows," he said, "that we will give whatever help we can to Russia and the Russian people. . . . It is not for me to speak of the action of the United States, but this I will say: If Hitler imagines that his attack on Soviet Russia will cause the slightest division of aims or slackening of effort in the great democracies, who are resolved upon his doom, he is woefully mistaken."

This was the British government pledging to the Soviet government indirect access to the American arsenal of democracy. And why not? It may do what it likes with the weapons and munitions it receives from that arsenal under the Lend-Lease Law; it may use them itself or lend them to others.

After the Churchill broadcast, which of course was directed at the American people, there could be no intelligent doubt about the policy of the American Government. Promptly on Monday the State Department restated the Churchill statement and presented it as its own to a "realistic America."

And the satirical thought—that, too, was very soon confirmed. On Sunday afternoon, from the office of the Communist Daily Worker, that had gone to press Saturday night praying for the Stalin-Hitler pact and breathing sabotage against the American armament program, the Communist Party issued a manifesto, saying the Soviet government was fighting not for itself alone but for the freedom of all people, including the American people—the American farmer, the American worker, the American Negro, and then, for good measure, even the hated middle class. Therefore, down with Hitler! All out for the American effort to destroy him—and save the Soviet Union! . . .

One of the sinister effects of the foreign malady is to make Americans suspect one another and impugn one another's patriotism. Many Americans were moved by both reason and deep feeling to say the Battle of Britain was our battle too. But to the voices of these were added alien voices saying the same thing in the same words, and their evangel for war was supported by an organized alien propaganda that could not have been thinking, and should not have been thinking, of America first.

Many more Americans—a great majority, we think—were equally moved by reason and feeling to say this country should jealously mind its own defense and stay out of the war, let Europe commit suicide if it would. That is the side we were on. But on that side, too, were alien voices saying the same thing in the same words. After a year it had become a habit, on opening the editorial mail, to glance first at the opening sentence of a letter, and if it was with us against going to war, to look then at the signature, and if it was a German name or any name we knew bearing the taint of Communism, we shuddered. Our answer was to wish those who might agree with us for wrong reasons to hold their peace.

The America First Committee made the same rejection; nevertheless, alien voices continued to embarrass its meetings, and Americans on the other side, together with their alien friends, made smear matter of it. Now the problem is theirs—how to repudiate the unwelcome support of the Communist.

Exercises in realistic thinking, now recommended by the American Government, were novel for a people who had just been brought to a crusade for the four freedoms in the wide world. Owing partly to the novelty, they were exciting and jammed all the channels of the air, alien voices intervening helpfully; but they were not easy, after all.

The Government was going to hit Hitler in the back with everything we had by sending it faster and faster to Great Britain, and at the same time it was going to aid Stalin with everything that was left over after we had sent everything to Great Britain; and if that was not clear, you had not yet learned to think in a realistic manner.

In *The New York Times*, Arthur Krock cynically resolved the difficulty of treating the Stalin dictatorship as a democracy for purposes of aid under the Lend-Lease Law by calling attention to the fact that Greece was not a democracy, nor China, except in a way of speaking.

In the House of Representatives, a member rose to ask why he should vote for a law forbidding any of the money the Congress was then appropriating to be used by the Government to pay the salaries of Communists employed in its various executive bureaus, some of them mentioned by name. What was the point?

We have produced this view of the formless national behavior only to prepare a question. Where in that view, or in any view you may construct for yourself out of the current materials, do you see America itself, or any true symbol of it?

In all this confusion of thought and feeling and idea, where is the American core?

Russian Communism is an international snake, treacherous even to itself, knowing only venomous and deadly enmity to any other kind of social organism. Nevertheless, the New Deal nested it. The White House made a fashion of petting it. Then just when the horrible awakening from this singular ophiolatry seemed about to take place—troops having been sent to dislodge the coil that had been trying to strangle the aircraft industry—a violent turn of events in Europe brings the Soviet government under the American tent of the four freedoms, and the short-wave listeners in a New York studio hear the Moscow radio playing "Columbia, the Gem of the Ocean and other patriotic American and Scottish songs."

Nazism is a similar reptile. Happily, now the Government is killing that one; and yet, even as to this well-doing, our satisfaction must be offset by the reflection that as the American Government puts down one kind of foreign propaganda it favors another kind, and does now itself collaborate with a foreign government in ways of acting upon mass opinion in the United States. And this, we suppose, is so far the extreme phase of the foreign malady among us, all the more critical because it is so little resented.

11.　Churchill and Roosevelt

THE ATLANTIC CHARTER

Roosevelt indeed went right on collaborating "with a foreign government in ways of acting upon mass opinion in the United States." In August, he met with Winston Churchill off the coast of Newfoundland. As a result of that meeting, Great Britain and the United States—though the latter still was technically neutral—issued this statement of joint war aims:

Source: *The Public Papers of Franklin D. Roosevelt*, Vol. X (Harper & Brothers, New York, 1950), pp. 314-315.

The President of the United States and the Prime Minister, Mr. Churchill, representing His Majesty's Government in the United Kingdom, have met at sea. . . .

The President and the Prime Minister have had several conferences. They have considered the dangers to world civilization arising from the policies of military domination and conquest upon which the Hitlerite Government of Germany and other Governments associated therewith have embarked and have made clear the steps which their countries are respectively taking for their safety in the face of these dangers.

They have agreed upon the following joint declaration:

The President of the United States of America and the Prime Minister, Mr. Churchill, representing His Majesty's Government in the United Kingdom, being met together, deem it right to make known certain common principles in the national policies of their respective countries on which they base their hopes for a better future for the world.

First, their countries seek no aggrandizement, territorial or other;

Second, they desire to see no territorial changes that do not accord with the freely expressed wishes of the peoples concerned;

Third, they respect the right of all peoples to choose the form of government under which they will live; and they wish to see sovereign rights and self-government restored to those who have been forcibly deprived of them;

Fourth, they will endeavor, with due respect for their existing obligations, to further the enjoyment by all states, great or small, victor or vanquished, of access, on equal terms, to the trade and to the raw materials of the world which are needed for their economic prosperity;

Fifth, they desire to bring about the fullest collaboration between all Nations in the economic field with the object of securing, for all, improved labor standards, economic advancement, and social security;

Sixth, after the final destruction of the Nazi tyranny, they hope to see established a peace which will afford to all Nations the means of dwelling in safety within their own boundaries, and which will afford assurance that all the men in all the lands may live out their lives in freedom from fear and want;

Seventh, such a peace should enable all men to traverse the high seas and oceans without hindrance;

Eighth, they believe that all of the Nations of the world, for realistic as well as spiritual reasons, must come to the abandonment of the use of force. Since no future peace can be maintained if land, sea, or air armaments continue to be employed by Nations which threaten, or may threaten, aggression outside of their frontiers, they believe, pending the establishment of a wider and permanent system of general security, that the disarmament of such Nations is essential. They will likewise aid and encourage all other practicable measures which will lighten for peace-loving peoples the crushing burden of armaments.

FRANKLIN D. ROOSEVELT
WINSTON S. CHURCHILL

August 14, 1941

12.   FRANKLIN D. ROOSEVELT

"THE RATTLESNAKES OF THE ATLANTIC"

Once more, talk was the prelude to action involving the United States even more deeply in the war. For some time, units of the American navy had helped in convoying British ships across the Atlantic. Inevitably, some American as well as British vessels had come under fire from German submarines. In September 1941, the American destroyer *Greer* was attacked by a German U-boat. It was, as the President conceded at a press conference, an unbloody attack; the torpedoes had missed their mark. What he did not mention, either at that press conference or in his subsequent message, was that the attack was not precisely unprovoked; before being fired on, the *Greer* had been trailing the U-boat.

In response, Roosevelt ordered the American navy to sink Axis submarines wherever it encountered them. In an address to the American public on September 11, 1941, he explained his action. It was, in a way, a reversal of the situation during World War I, when German submarines, by firing first and without warning, had provoked the United States into entering the war. This time, it was the Americans who would shoot on sight.

Source: The Public Papers of Franklin D. Roosevelt, Vol. X, pp. 384-392.

The Navy Department of the United States has reported to me that on the morning of September fourth the United States destroyer *Greer*, proceeding in full daylight toward Iceland, had reached a point southeast of Greenland. She was carrying American mail to Iceland. She was flying the American flag. Her identity as an American ship was unmistakable.

She was then and there attacked by a submarine. Germany admits that it was a German submarine. The submarine deliberately fired a torpedo at the *Greer*, followed later by another torpedo attack. In spite of what Hitler's propaganda bureau has invented, and in spite of what any American obstructionist organization may prefer to believe, I tell you the blunt fact that the German submarine fired first upon this American destroyer without warning, and with deliberate design to sink her.

Our destroyer, at the time, was in waters which the Government of the United States had declared to be waters of self-defense—surrounding outposts of American protection in the Atlantic.

In the North of the Atlantic, outposts have been established by us in Iceland, in Greenland, in Labrador and in Newfoundland. Through these waters there pass many ships of many flags. They bear food and other supplies to civilians; and they bear matériel of war, for which the people of the United States are spending billions of dollars, and which, by Congressional action, they have declared to be essential for the defense of our own land.

The United States destroyer, when attacked, was proceeding on a legitimate mission. . . .

This was piracy—piracy legally and morally. It was not the first nor the last act of piracy which the Nazi Government has committed against the American flag in this war. For attack has followed attack. . . .

The important truth is that these acts of international lawlessness are a manifestation of a design which has been made clear to the American people for a long time. It is the Nazi design to abolish the freedom of the seas, and to acquire absolute control and domination of these seas for themselves.

For with control of the seas in their own hands, the way can obviously become clear for their next step—domination of the United States—domination of the Western Hemisphere by force of arms. Under Nazi control of the seas, no merchant ship of the United States or of any other American Republic would be free to carry on any peaceful commerce, except by the condescending grace of this foreign and tyrannical power. The Atlantic Ocean which has been, and which should always be, a free and friendly highway for us would then become a deadly menace to the commerce of the United States, to the coasts of the United States, and even to the inland cities of the United States.

The Hitler Government, in defiance of the laws of the sea, in defiance of the recognized rights of all other Nations, has presumed to declare, on paper, that great areas of the seas—even including a vast expanse lying in the Western Hemisphere—are to be closed, and that no ships may enter them for any purpose, except at peril of being sunk. Actually they are sinking ships at will and without warning in widely separated areas both within and far outside of these far-flung pretended zones.

This Nazi attempt to seize control of the oceans is but a counterpart of the Nazi plots now being carried on throughout the Western Hemisphere—all designed toward the same end. For Hitler's advance guards—not only his avowed agents but also his dupes among us—have sought to make ready for him footholds and bridgeheads in the New World, to be used as soon as he has gained control of the oceans. . . .

To be ultimately successful in world mastery, Hitler knows that he must get control of the seas. He must first destroy the bridge of ships which we are building across the Atlantic and over which we shall continue to roll the implements of war to help destroy him, to destroy all his works in the end. He must wipe out our patrol on sea and in the air if he is to do it. He must silence the British Navy.

I think it must be explained over and over again to people who like to think of the United States Navy as an invincible protection, that this can be true only if the British Navy survives. And that, my friends, is simple arithmetic.

For if the world outside of the Americas falls under Axis domination, the shipbuilding facilities which the Axis powers would then possess in all of Europe, in the British Isles, and in the Far East would be much greater than all the shipbuilding facilities and potentialities of all of the Americas—not only greater, but two or three times greater—enough to win. Even if the United States threw all its resources into such a situation, seeking to double and even redouble the size of our Navy, the Axis powers, in control of the rest of the world, would have the manpower and the physical resources to outbuild us several times over.

It is time for all Americans, Americans of all the Americas to stop being deluded by the romantic notion that the Americas can go on living happily and peacefully in a Nazi-dominated world. . . .

The Nazi danger to our Western world has long ceased to be a mere possibility. The danger is here now—not only from a military enemy but from an enemy of all law, all liberty, all morality, all religion.

There has now come a time when you and I must see the cold, inexorable necessity of saying to these inhuman, unrestrained seekers of world conquest and permanent world domination by the sword: "You seek to throw our children and our children's children into your form of terrorism and slavery. You have now attacked our own safety. You shall go no further." . . .

We have sought no shooting war with Hitler. We do not seek it now. But neither do we want peace so much, that we are willing to pay for it by permitting him to attack our naval and merchant ships while they are on legitimate business.

I assume that the German leaders are not deeply concerned, tonight or any other time, by what we Americans or the American Government say or publish about them. We cannot bring about the downfall of Nazism by the use of long-range invective.

But when you see a rattlesnake poised to strike, you do not wait until he has struck before you crush him.

These Nazi submarines and raiders are the rattlesnakes of the Atlantic. They are a menace to the free pathways of the high seas. They are a challenge to our sovereignty. They hammer at our most precious rights when they attack ships of the American flag—symbols of our independence, our freedom, our very life. . . .

It is no act of war on our part when we decide to protect the seas that are vital to American defense. The aggression is not ours. Ours is solely defense.

But let this warning be clear. From now on, if German or Italian vessels of war enter the waters, the protection of which is necessary for American defense, they do so at their own peril.

The orders which I have given as Commander in Chief of the United States Army and Navy are to carry out that policy—at once.

The sole responsibility rests upon Germany. There will be no shooting unless Germany continues to seek it.

That is my obvious duty in this crisis. That is the clear right of this sovereign Nation. This is the only step possible, if we would keep tight the wall of defense which we are pledged to maintain around this Western Hemisphere.

I have no illusions about the gravity of this step. I have not taken it hurriedly or lightly. It is the result of months and months of constant thought and anxiety and prayer. In the protection of your Nation and mine it cannot be avoided.

The American people have faced other grave crises in their history—with American courage, and with American resolution. They will do no less today.

They know the actualities of the attacks upon us. They know the necessities of a bold defense against these attacks. They know that the times call for clear heads and fearless hearts.

And with that inner strength that comes to a free people conscious of their duty, and conscious of the righteousness of what they do, they will—with Divine help and guidance—stand their ground against this latest assault upon their democracy, their sovereignty, and their freedom.

13.

DRAFT PROPOSAL HANDED BY THE JAPANESE AMBASSADOR TO THE SECRETARY OF STATE

It was, as one American historian put it, "the beginning of *de facto* war in the Atlantic." Yet full-scale war, when it came, would come not in the Atlantic but in the Pacific, would result not from the conflict with Germany but from that with Japan.

Source: Papers Relating to the Foreign Relations of the United States, Japan: 1931–1941 (United States Government Printing Office, Washington, D.C., 1943), Vol. II, pp. 753 and 755–756.

Japan's moves to profit from the war in Europe, and to expand into Southeast Asia and China, had long been accompanied by American counter-moves. It seemed in the United States' interest to support an independent China, and to maintain the American sphere of influence in the Pacific. In the beginning, the effort to check Japan's expansion took the form of moral condemnation and of verbal warnings, but—and here the story of European appeasement was not repeated—these were quickly followed by economic reprisals. There was the restrictive licensing of oil and scrap metals to Japan in July 1940, accompanied by an embargo on the export of aviation gasoline. In September of that year, in response to Japan's occupation of Indo-China, exports of scrap iron and steel were halted entirely. Ten months later, with Japan allied to Germany and Italy in the Tripartite pact, Roosevelt decided on even stronger measures. By executive order, all Japanese assets in the United States were frozen. It was an action that effectively halted any trade between the United States and Japan, including oil shipments considered vital by the Japanese.

The effect on Japan was to strengthen the forces that wished war with the United States. Prince Konoye, who had favored a peaceful arrangement with Washington, was replaced as prime minister by General Hideki Tojo, who weighted his new government with military members. Yet Tojo still hesitated before taking the ultimate step. Rather than rushing into action, he pursued a policy of "dual initiative"—of preparing for war, yet trying to halt it by a final effort at diplomatic compromise. Suburu Kurusu, an experienced Japanese diplomat (it was Kurusu who had signed the Tripartite pact in Berlin the preceding year) was sent to Washington to assist Ambassador Nomura, who felt somewhat out of touch with the new Tojo government, in negotiating a last-minute settlement. On November 20, 1941, the two ambassadors called on the American secretary of state, Cordell Hull, to submit that last offer for a *modus vivendi:* Japanese territorial restraint in Southeast Asia for the resumption of American trade.

[WASHINGTON,] November 20, 1941.

The Japanese Ambassador and Mr. Kurusu called at their request at the Department. Mr. Kurusu said that they had referred to their Government the suggestion which the Ambassador had made at a previous meeting in regard to a return to the status which prevailed prior to the Japanese move into south Indochina last July, and said that they had anticipated that the Japanese Government might perceive difficulty in moving troops out of Indochina in short order, but that nevertheless the Japanese Government was now prepared to offer a proposal on that basis. He said, however, that the proposal represented an amplification of the Ambassador's suggestion. He then read the proposal to the Secretary which was as follows:

1. Both the Governments of Japan and the United States undertake not to make any armed advancement into any of the regions in the South-eastern Asia and the Southern Pacific area excepting the part of French Indo-China where the Japanese troops are stationed at present.

2. The Japanese Government undertakes to withdraw its troops now stationed in French Indo-China upon either the restoration of peace between Japan and China or the establishment of an equitable peace in the Pacific area.

   In the meantime the Government of Japan declares that it is prepared to remove its troops now stationed in the southern part of French Indo-China to the northern part of the said territory upon the conclusion of the present arrangement which shall later be embodied in the final agreement.

3. The Government of Japan and the United States shall cooperate with a view to securing the acquisition of those goods and commodities which the two countries need in Netherlands East Indies.

4. The Governments of Japan and the United States mutually undertake to restore their commercial relations to those prevailing prior to the freezing of the assets.

   The Government of the United States shall supply Japan a required quantity of oil.

5. The Government of the United States undertakes to refrain from such measures and actions as will be prejudicial to the endeavors for the restoration of general peace between Japan and China.

The Secretary said that he would later examine the proposal, and that he would give sympathetic study to the proposal speaking generally, but that the comments which he was about to make were not directed specifically to the proposal but to the general situation. The Secretary said that Japan had it in its power at any moment to put an end to the present situation by deciding upon an all-out peaceful course; that at any moment Japan could bring to an end what Japan chose to call encirclement. He said that we want to have Japan develop public opinion in favor of a peaceful course. Mr. Kurusu said that if we could alleviate the situation by adopting a proposal such as the Japanese Government had just made it would help develop public opinion. . . .

14.

THE JAPANESE FOREIGN MINISTRY TO THE WASHINGTON EMBASSY

That this was no routine communication was apparent both from the text itself and from the circumstances of its delivery. But it was apparent for another reason as well. Ever since the summer of 1941, Washington officials had been able to read the most secret communications between Tokyo and its diplomats, since in an operation known as "Magic," the Japanese code had been broken. Among the intercepted telegrams were the two that are printed here. They could leave little doubt that should negotiations fail, the Japanese were committed to war, and committed to it by a fixed timetable.

From: Tokyo
To: Washington
5 November 1941
(Purple—CA)
#736

(Of utmost secrecy).

Because of various circumstances, it is absolutely necessary that all arrangements for the signing of this agreement be completed by the 25th of this month. I realize that this is a difficult order, but under the circumstances it is an unavoidable one. Please understand this thoroughly and tackle the problem of saving the Japanese-U. S. relations from falling into a chaotic condition. Do so with great determination and with unstinted effort, I beg of you.

This information is to be kept strictly to yourself only.

24373   (D) Navy Trans. 11-5-41 (S-TT)
JD—1:6254

Source: Congress of the United States, *Hearings Before The Joint Committee on the Investigation of the Pearl Harbor Attack*, Part 12, Exhibits Nos. 1 through 6 (U. S. Government Printing Office, Washington, D.C., 1946), pp. 100 and 165.

Secret
From: Tokyo
To: Washington
November 22, 1941
Purple CA (Urgent)
#812

To both you Ambassadors.

It is awfully hard for us to consider changing the date we set in my #736. You should know this, however, I know you are working hard. Stick to our fixed policy and do your very best. Spare no efforts and try to bring about the solution we desire. There are reasons beyond your ability to guess why we wanted to settle Japanese-American relations by the 25th, but if within the next three or four days you can finish your conversations with the Americans; if the signing can be completed by the 29th, (let me write it out for you—twenty ninth); if the pertinent notes can be exchanged; if we can get an understanding with Great Britain and the Netherlands; and in short if everything can be finished, we have decided to wait until that date. This time we mean it, that the deadline absolutely cannot be changed. After that things are automatically going to happen. Please take this into your careful consideration and work harder than you ever have before. This, for the present, is for the information of you two Ambassadors alone.

Army 25138   Trans. 11/22/41 (S)

15.

A NOTE HANDED TO THE SECRETARY OF STATE BY THE JAPANESE AMBASSADOR

Yet the American counter-proposal, submitted about a week later, asked for a very great deal more than the Japanese had offered—including the withdrawal of all Japanese forces from China and Indo-China, and a virtual diplomatic realignment, providing for a nonaggression pact between Japan and the Western allies. The Japanese offer had, in effect, been rejected.

MEMORANDUM OF A CONVERSATION

[WASHINGTON,] November 26, 1941.

The Japanese Ambassador and Mr. Kurusu called by appointment at the Department. The Secretary handed each of the Japanese copies of an outline of a proposed basis of an agreement between the United States and Japan and an explanatory oral statement.

After the Japanese had read the documents, Mr. Kurusu asked whether this was our reply to their proposal for a *modus vivendi*. The Secretary replied that we had to treat the proposal as we did, as there was so much turmoil and confusion among the public both in the United States and in Japan. He reminded the Japanese that in the United States we have a political situation to deal with just as does the Japanese Government, and he referred to thefire-eating statements which have been recently coming out of Tokyo, which he said had been causing a natural reaction among the public in this country. . . .

The Ambassador took the occasion to observe that sometimes statesmen of firm conviction fail to get sympathizers among the public; that only wise men could see far ahead and sometimes suffered martyrdom; but that life's span was short and one could only do his duty. The Ambassador then asked whether there was no other possibility and whether they could not see the President.

Source: Foreign Relations, Japan, Vol. II, pp. 764–770.

The Secretary replied that he had no doubt that the President would be glad to see them at any time.

Mr. Kurusu said that he felt that our response to their proposal could be interpreted as tantamount to meaning the end, and asked whether we were not interested in a *modus vivendi.*

The Secretary replied that we had explored that. Mr. Kurusu asked whether it was because the other powers would not agree; but the Secretary replied simply that he had done his best in the way of exploration. . . .

DOCUMENT HANDED BY THE SECRETARY OF STATE
TO THE JAPANESE AMBASSADOR (NOMURA)
ON NOVEMBER 26, 1941

Strictly Confidential,
Tentative and Without
Commitment.   WASHINGTON, November 26, 1941.

OUTLINE OF PROPOSED BASIS FOR AGREEMENT BETWEEN THE UNITED STATES AND JAPAN

SECTION I

DRAFT MUTUAL DECLARATION OF POLICY

The Government of the United States and the Government of Japan both being solicitous for the peace of the Pacific affirm that their national policies are directed toward lasting and extensive peace throughout the Pacific area, that they have no territorial designs in that area, that they have no intention of threatening other countries or of using military force aggressively against any neighboring nation, and that, accordingly, in their national policies they will actively support and give practical application to the following fundamental principles upon which their relations with each other and with all other governments are based:

> (1) The principle of inviolability of territorial integrity and sovereignty of each and all nations.

(2) The principle of non-interference in the internal affairs of other countries.

(3) The principle of equality, including equality of commercial opportunity and treatment.

(4) The principle of reliance upon international cooperation and conciliation for the prevention and pacific settlement of controversies and for improvement of international conditions by peaceful methods and processes.

The Government of Japan and the Government of the United States have agreed that toward eliminating chronic political instability, preventing recurrent economic collapse, and providing a basis for peace, they will actively support and practically apply the following principles in their economic relations with each other and with other nations and peoples:

(1) The principle of non-discrimination in international commercial relations.

(2) The principle of international economic cooperation and abolition of extreme nationalism as expressed in excessive trade restrictions.

(3) The principle of non-discriminatory access by all nations to raw material supplies.

(4) The principle of full protection of the interests of consuming countries and populations as regards the operation of international commodity agreements.

(5) The principle of establishment of such institutions and arrangements of international finance as may lend aid to the essential enterprises and the continuous development of all countries and may permit payments through processes of trade consonant with the welfare of all countries.

SECTION II

STEPS TO BE TAKEN BY THE GOVERNMENT OF THE UNITED STATES AND BY THE GOVERNMENT OF JAPAN

The Government of the United States and the Government of Japan propose to take steps as follows:

1. The Government of the United States and the Government of Japan will endeavor to conclude a multilateral non-aggression pact among the British Empire, China, Japan, the Netherlands, the Soviet Union, Thailand and the United States.

2. Both Governments will endeavor to conclude among the American, British, Chinese, Japanese, the Netherland and Thai Governments an agreement whereunder each of the Governments would pledge itself to respect the territorial integrity of French Indochina and, in the event that there should develop a threat to the territorial integrity of Indochina, to enter into immediate consultation with a view to taking such measures as may be deemed necessary and advisable to meet the threat in question. Such agreement would provide also that each of the Governments party to the agreement would not seek or accept preferential treatment in its trade or economic relations with Indochina and would use its influence to obtain for each of the signatories equality of treatment in trade and commerce with French Indochina.

3. The Government of Japan will withdraw all military, naval, air and police forces from China and from Indochina.

4. The Government of the United States and the Government of Japan will not support—militarily, politically, economically— any government or regime in China other than the National Government of the Republic of China with capital temporarily at Chungking.

5. Both Governments will give up all extraterritorial rights in China, including rights and interests in and with regard to international settlements and concessions, and rights under the Boxer Protocol of 1901.

Both Governments will endeavor to obtain the agreement of the British and other governments to give up extraterritorial rights in China, including rights in international settlements and in concessions and under the Boxer Protocol of 1901.

6. The Government of the United States and the Government of Japan will enter into negotiations for the conclusion between the United States and Japan of a trade agreement, based upon reciprocal most-favored-nation treatment and reduction of trade barriers by both countries, including an undertaking by the United States to bind raw silk on the free list.

7. The Government of the United States and the Government of Japan will, respectively, remove the freezing restrictions on

Japanese funds in the United States and on American funds in Japan.

8. Both Governments will agree upon a plan for the stabilization of the dollar-yen rate, with the allocation of funds adequate for this purpose, half to be supplied by Japan and half by the United States.

9. Both Governments will agree that no agreement which either has concluded with any third power or powers shall be interpreted by it in such a way as to conflict with the fundamental purpose of this agreement, the establishment and preservation of peace throughout the Pacific area.

10. Both Governments will use their influence to cause other governments to adhere to and to give practical application to the basic political and economic principles set forth in this agreement.

16.

MEMORANDUM BY SECRETARY OF STATE HULL

The next day, the meeting with the president which the Japanese had requested took place. It changed nothing.

[WASHINGTON] November 27, 1941.

The two Japanese Ambassadors called at their request. The President opened the conversation with some reference to German international psychology. Ambassador Nomura then said that they were disappointed about the failure of any agreement regarding a *modus vivendi*. The President proceeded to express the grateful appreciation of himself and of this Government to the peace element in Japan which has worked hard in support of the movement to establish a peaceful settlement in the Pacific area. He made it clear that we were not overlooking for a moment what that element has done and is ready still to do. The President added that

Source: Foreign Relations, Japan, Vol. II, pp. 770–772.

in the United States most people want a peaceful solution of all matters in the Pacific area. He said that he does not give up yet although the situation is serious and that fact should be recognized. He then referred to the conversations since April which have been carried on here with the Japanese Ambassador in an attempt to deal with the difficulties. The President added that some of these difficulties at times have the effect of a cold bath on the United States Government and people, such as the recent occupation of Indochina by the Japanese and recent movements and utterances of the Japanese slanting wholly in the direction of conquest by force and ignoring the whole question of a peaceful settlement and the principles underlying it. . . .

Ambassador Kurusu proceeded to say that he had been here for ten days in an endeavor to discuss and develop a peaceful arrangement; that the trouble was not with the fundamentals so much as with their application. . . .

The President, referring to the efforts of Japan to colonize countries that they conquer, said that Germany would completely fail because she did not have enough top people to govern the fifteen or more conquered countries in Europe and that this would cause Germany to fail in her present movements; that second class people cannot run fifteen captured countries.

The President further referred to the matter of encirclement that Japan has been alleging. He pointed out that the Philippines were being encircled by Japan so far as that is concerned.

I made it clear that unless the opposition to the peace element in control of the Government should make up its mind definitely to act and talk and move in a peaceful direction, no conversations could or would get anywhere as has been so clearly demonstrated; that everyone knows that the Japanese slogans of co-prosperity, new order in East Asia and a controlling influence in certain areas, are all terms to express in a camouflaged manner the policy of force and conquest by Japan and the domination by military agencies of the political, economic, social and moral affairs of each of the populations conquered; and that so long as they move in that direction and continue to increase their cultural relations, military and otherwise with Hitler through such instruments as the Anti-Comintern Pact and the Tripartite Pact, et cetera, et cetera, there could not be any real progress made on a peaceful course.

C[ORDELL] H[ULL]

17.

THE JAPANESE FOREIGN MINISTRY TO THE WASHINGTON EMBASSY AND THE HAVANA LEGATION

It was over. If there had been the least lingering doubts in the minds of those who made American policy of how unacceptable their proposal was to the Japanese, it was dispelled by the secret Japanese messages intercepted and decoded under operation "Magic."

Secret

From: Tokyo
To: Washington
November 28, 1941.
Purple (CA)
#844

Re your #1189

Well, you two Ambassadors have exerted superhuman efforts but, in spite of this, the United States has gone ahead and presented this humiliating proposal. This was quite unexpected and extremely regrettable. The Imperial Government can by no means use it as a basis for negotiations. Therefore, with a report of the views of the Imperial Government on this American proposal which I will send you in two or three days, the negotiations will be de facto ruptured. This is inevitable. However, I do not wish you to give the impression that the negotiations are broken off. Merely say to them that you are awaiting instructions and that, although the opinions of your Government are not yet clear to you, to your own way of thinking the Imperial Government has always made just claims and has borne great sacrifices for the sake of peace in the Pacific. Say that we have always demonstrated a long-suffering and conciliatory attitude, but that, on the other hand, the United States has been unbending, making it impossible for Japan to establish negotiations. Since things have come to this pass, I contacted the man you told me to in your #1180[1] and he said that under the present cir-

Source: Hearings Before the Joint Committee on the Investigation of the Pearl Harbor Attack, Part 12, pp. 195 and 215–216.
[1] The Minister of the Navy.

cumstances what you suggest is entirely unsuitable. From now on do the best you can.

Army 25445
JD 6898   Trans. 11–28–41 (S)

From: Tokyo (Togo)
To: Washington
December 2, 1941
Purple

CORRECTED TRANSLATION

#867.   (Strictly Secret)

1. Among the telegraphic codes with which your office is equipped burn all but those now used with the machine and one copy each of "O" code (Oite) and abbreviating code (L). (Burn also the various other codes which you have in your custody.)

2. Stop at once using one code machine unit and destroy it completely.

3. When you have finished this, wire me back the one word "haruna."

4. At the time and in the manner you deem most proper dispose of all files of messages coming and going and all other secret documents.

5. Burn all the codes which Telegraphic Official KOSAKA brought you. . . .

Army 25640   Translated 12–3–41 (X) Corrected 12–4–41

From: Tokyo (Togo)
To: Havana
December 2, 1941
J 19–K 9
Circular #2445   Strictly secret.

Take great pains that this does not leak out.

You are to take the following measures immediately:

1. With the exception of one copy of the O and L code, you are to burn all telegraph codes (this includes the code books for

communication between the three departments and the code books for Army and Navy communication).

2. As soon as you have completed this operation, wire the one word Haruna.

3. Burn all secret documents and the work sheets on this message.

4. Be especially careful not to arouse the suspicion of those on the outside. Confidential documents are all to be given the same handling.

The above is preparatory to an emergency situation and is for your information alone. Remain calm. . . .

Army 25879   Transl. 12/41 (3)

18.   DEAN ACHESON

MEMOIRS

Initially, staying calm seemed to be Washington's motto, too. That the Japanese were about to strike was known, but precisely where they would strike was not. (It was a problem that bothered Roosevelt. According to Secretary of War Stimson, the president told a few intimates at the end of November about an impending Japanese attack, adding that the "question was how we should maneuver them into the position of firing the first shot without allowing too much danger to ourselves. It was a difficult problem.")

"Magic" notwithstanding, there had been some secrets that the Japanese managed to keep to themselves. Hence, when it turned out that Pearl Harbor was the target, calm was replaced by considerable confusion in Washington. Later, historians would write that the Pearl Harbor attack made the war into a global one, and that once it was that, the ultimate chances of the Tripartite powers' winning it were slim. But on December 7, 1941, things were rather less clear and neat. Dean Acheson, then an assistant secretary of state, recorded some of the scene.

Source: Dean Acheson, *Present at the Creation, My Years in the State Department* (W. W. Norton & Company, New York, 1969), pp. 34–35.

SUNDAY, DECEMBER 7

On Sunday, December 7, Archie and Ada MacLeish drove out to our Maryland farm north of Washington to get some exercise by clearing up fallen timber in our woods and to share a picnic lunch. He was then Librarian of Congress and head of the "Office of Facts and Figures," FDR's ingenious name for our foreign propaganda bureau. The MacLeishes had to get back to town for an afternoon appointment and left us soon after lunch. In a few minutes Archie was running down the hill from the house shouting, "The Japanese have attacked Pearl Harbor. Turn on your car radio." Then he was gone.

We soon followed him, listening to reports of unbelievable disaster as we drove. I dropped off at the Department. On the second floor south little groups stood about the corridor, talking almost in whispers, doing nothing. Mr. Hull was shut up with a few intimates, still, it was reported, in a towering rage. The Japanese Ambassador, Admiral Kichisaburo Nomura, and their special ambassador, Saburo Kurusu, had left him only a couple of hours before. Each group added its bit of gossip. Mr. Hull had reportedly castigated the departing envoys in native Tennesseean as "scoundrels and piss-ants." War had or had not been declared. Germany would or would not join Japan. The axis plan was or was not to involve us in the Pacific leaving the European partners a free hand to finish the European war first; and so on. Our Petroleum Adviser, Max Thornburg, reported having seen terrifying telegraphed photographs of our shattered fleet. When no one seemed to have any use or orders for us, the groups dissolved and we went home.

HITLER'S REACTION
TO PEARL HARBOR

For the briefest of moments, there was some question of whether the Japanese would be joined in war by their European treaty partners. The Tripartite pact, after all, was more verbal than real, and the Pearl Harbor attack had come as a surprise to Berlin and Rome as much as to Washington. (The Germans, for their part, had been no more communicative about their intentions. "No hint of Operation Barbarossa [the plaenned campaign against Russia] must be given to the Japanese," read a Hitler instruction of September 1940.) But the question was quickly resolved, as the declarations of war passed between Berlin, Rome, and Washington. Erich Kordt, who as one of the chief aides to the German foreign minister, von Ribbentrop, was something of Dean Acheson's counterpart in Berlin, recorded how between them, Hitler's action in eastern Europe and Japan's in the Pacific had now brought about the century's second world war.

Hitler received the news of the attack on Pearl Harbor in his headquarters in the Ukraine. He was beside himself with joy, and immediately gave his approval for the conclusion of a new Tripartite pact on the joint conduct of the war, which was signed on December 11 in Berlin in his presence by Ribbentrop, Ciano,[1] and Ambassador Oshima. As early as December 8, Ribbentrop had told Oshima that Hitler had ordered all American shipping, no matter where it was encountered, to be attacked forthwith. The same day, Oshima reported to Tokyo that Germany and Italy intended to declare war on the United States. The Japanese foreign ministry was much relieved; in view of the clearly aggressive nature of Japan's action, they had been somewhat worried about the attitude that their allies would take.

Ribbentrop told Oshima that Hitler felt that in effect, a state of war had existed ever since the shoot-on-sight order of September 11. Ribbentrop told his intimates, "A great power like Germany declares war, it does not wait until somebody else declares it." . . .

Source: Kordt, *Wahn und Wirklichkeit*, p. 332 (translated by the editor).
[1] Mussolini's foreign minister.

Suggestions for Further Reading

The best general accounts of the coming of the war, from the aftermath of Versailles to the invasion of Poland, are KEITH EUBANK, *The Origins of World War II* (New York, 1969), and LAURENCE LAFORE, *The End of Glory, An Interpretation of the Origins of World War II* (Philadelphia, 1970). Another, earlier book on the topic, A. J. P. TAYLOR, *The Origins of the Second World War* (London, 1961) is readable but eccentric. It may profitably be balanced by WALTHER HOFER's readable and solid *War Premeditated, 1939* (London, 1955), as well as by the first volume of NORMAN RICH, *Hitler's War Aims* (New York, 1973), which offers as informed and clear a discussion as any of why and how the war grew out of Hitler's plans. A detailed narrative, elegantly handled, of the final diplomatic crises that preceded the war is CHRISTOPHER THORNE, *The Approach of War, 1938–1939* (New York, 1967), as is the more recent SIDNEY ASTER, *1939: The Making of the Second World War* (New York, 1974).

A number of good books deal with appeasement, mostly from the British side, and often in a way that is critical of Chamberlain and his policies. Particularly notable among them are KEITH EU-BANK, *Munich* (Norman, 1963); MARTIN GILBERT, *The Roots of Appeasement* (London, 1966); MARTIN GILBERT and RICHARD GOTT, *The Appeasers* (London, 1963); KEITH ROBBINS, *Munich 1938* (London, 1968); and JOHN WHEELER-BENNETT, *Munich, Prologue to Tragedy* (London, 1948). GORDON A. CRAIG and FELIX GILBERT, eds., *The Diplomats: 1919–1939* (Princeton, 1953), contains some first-rate essays on several of the major figures involved; and similarly worth consulting are longer biographies such as KEITH FEILING, *The Life of Neville Chamberlain* (London, 1947) and IAIN MACLEOD, *Neville Chamberlain* (New York, 1962), or the memoirs of the various statesmen, and their assistants, of the period, such as WINSTON CHURCHILL, *The Second World War* (Boston, 1948–53); ANTHONY EDEN, *Facing the Dictators* (Boston, 1962); HAROLD MACMILLAN, *Winds of Change* (New York, 1966); BARON VANSITTART, *The Mist Procession* (London, 1958); or, for the German side, PAUL SCHMIDT, *Hitler's Interpreter* (London, 1951), a book that delivers more than its title promises.

The various crises of the time have produced a large and often distinguished literature of their own by now. Some of the outstanding titles are GABRIEL JACKSON, *The Spanish Republic and the*

Civil War, 1931–1939 (Princeton, 1967); ROBERT PAYNE, ed., *The Civil War in Spain, 1936–1939* (New York, 1970); HUGH THOMAS, *The Spanish Civil War* (New York, 1961); GEORGE W. BAER, *The Coming of the Italian-Ethiopian War* (Cambridge, 1967); GORDON BROOK-SHEPHERD, *The Anschluss* (New York, 1963); and GEORGE F. KENNAN, *From Prague after Munich: Diplomatic Papers 1938–1940* (Princeton, 1968).

On the extension of the war, three older books, for all the additional evidence that has appeared since they have, are still very much worth reading. One is GERHARD WEINBERG, *Germany and the Soviet Union, 1939–1941* (Leyden, 1954); the other two are HERBERT FEIS, *The Road to Pearl Harbor* (Princeton, 1950), and PAUL SCHROEDER, *The Axis Alliance and Japanese-American Relations* (Ithaca, 1958). The point that Schroeder in particular makes about the fragile nature of the Berlin-Tokyo ties is well borne out by JOHANNA MENZEL MESKILL, *Hitler and Japan, The Hollow Alliance* (New York, 1966).

On the war itself, the two most impressive general accounts are SIR BASIL LIDDELL HART, *History of the Second World War* (London, 1970), and GORDON WRIGHT, *The Ordeal of Total War, 1939–1945* (New York, 1968). Noteworthy too are J.F.C. FULLER, *The Second World War, 1939–1945: A Strategical and Tactical History* (New York, 1949); MARTHA BYRD HOYLE, *A World in Flames, A History of World War II* (New York, 1970); LOUIS L. SNYDER, *The War: A Concise History, 1939–1945* (New York, 1952); CHESTER WILMOT, *The Struggle for Europe* (New York, 1952); PETER YOUNG, *World War, 1939–45, A Short History* (London, 1966); and for America's part, A. RUSSELL BUCHANAN, ed., *The United States and World War II* (New York, 1972).

These titles are few and selective; a complete bibliography of the topic would take up more pages than this whole book has. But anyone interested in more detailed study is referred to the bibliographical essay in GORDON WRIGHT's *Ordeal of Total War*, with its succinct and sensible discussion of all the major books that appeared up until the late 1960s, and to the relevant entries in BYRON DEXTER, ed., *The Foreign Affairs 50-Year Bibliography* (New York, 1972). For studies that have appeared since then, there are the truly encyclopedic listings of the American Committee on the History of the Second World War, published at the University of Florida.

For maps of Japan and Europe see the following pages.

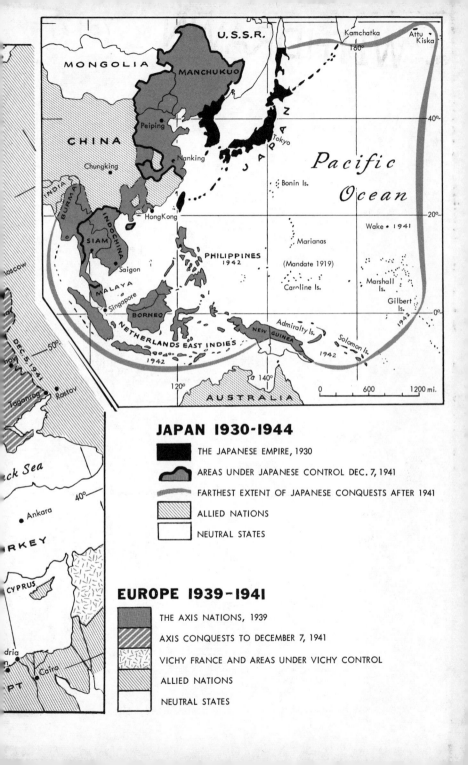

JAPAN 1930-1944

■ THE JAPANESE EMPIRE, 1930

▬ AREAS UNDER JAPANESE CONTROL DEC. 7, 1941

▬ FARTHEST EXTENT OF JAPANESE CONQUESTS AFTER 1941

▧ ALLIED NATIONS

☐ NEUTRAL STATES

EUROPE 1939-1941

▬ THE AXIS NATIONS, 1939

▧ AXIS CONQUESTS TO DECEMBER 7, 1941

▒ VICHY FRANCE AND AREAS UNDER VICHY CONTROL

▧ ALLIED NATIONS

☐ NEUTRAL STATES